GREAT PAINTINGS

IN AMERICA

GREAT PAINTINGS
IN AMERICA

ONE HUNDRED AND ONE MASTERPIECES IN COLOR

SELECTED AND INTERPRETED BY

FISKE KIMBALL

Director of the Philadelphia Museum of Art

AND

LIONELLO VENTURI

Professor of the History of Art at the University of Rome

COWARD-McCANN, INC.
New York

Manufactured in the United States of America

Produced by THE BECK ENGRAVING COMPANY · *Bound by* RUSSELL-RUTTER COMPANY, INC.

PREFACE

A new avenue to the enjoyment and knowledge of art has been opened by the development of processes of color reproduction. Until a few years ago these were limited to relatively expensive methods, which still left their products beyond the reach of the broad public. Improvement of the method of four-color letterpress printing has lately reached a point where we may hope for a public for great paintings as extensive as the audience the phonograph and the radio have gained for great music.

This book is published in the faith that, as in music, the American public in art is prepared today to respond to the highest and best which this country affords. The day is over when we need suppose that "what the public wants" is anything short of this. The day is over, too, when what America offers in art is only the second best. This book is equally an affirmation that in America today are to be found works of painting of the highest quality extending widely over time and space—works of which the reader may see the originals without leaving his own country.

Only a few realms of painting remain inaccessible to us in American museums, realms perhaps destined always to remain so. Fresco painting, which glorified the walls of Italy in the Renaissance, must, with few exceptions, remain there. Its greatest masters, Giotto and Masaccio, Leonardo and Michelangelo can doubtless never be seen fully except on these walls. Their easel paintings are few. Those of Leonardo and Michelangelo in the whole world can be counted on one's fingers. A very few other painters of leading rank are not represented in this country by indubitable works in pristine condition. In a few instances the best America offers are works from the atelier of the artist. Of all other supreme masters America now offers characteristic works, sometimes masterpieces among their very finest. For certain painters there is even an embarrassment of riches: the trends of American collecting offer a multitude of superb works of El Greco, of Rembrandt, of Vermeer, of the Impressionists, of Cézanne, of Renoir, for instance, among which even liberal selection must be arbitrary.

Even today the initial expense of producing fine color reproductions is staggering. The temptation, in making such a book as this, is to limit its contents to works of which color plates happen already to be available. The publisher and authors here have been determined to accept no compromise, but to make their choice representative of the history of art in examples as fine as may be found on this side of the ocean.

The task of choosing, from the present wealth of American collections, a selection of a hundred masterpieces of the history of painting is not an easy one. More than a hundred painters are of a stature which makes one regret that all cannot be included. Few artists, whatever their stature, can receive more than a single plate.

In a few cities, a few museums and collections, are concentrated more than a proportionate share of masterpieces, and their wealth is reflected inevitably in this volume. Nevertheless, in the effort to show paintings of which the originals may be seen in every quarter of the land, we have, where merit is equal, given preference to works in other cities than these. No region, no few museums, have a monopoly of quality.

In general, we have given preference to works in museums or collections regularly accessible to the public, but there are exceptions to this rule where it has seemed wise to include examples in private possession. The distinction is less important than it might be in some other countries, because of the liberality of American collectors in lending their treasures to exhibitions and in bequeathing them ultimately, with a unanimity quite unequalled elsewhere, for the enjoyment of the public at large. There were very few instances in which, from past experience, one could not count confidently, as the event has proved, that a request to include such works would be honored.

The two authors are fully at one in their view of the nature of art as individual creation, and in the selection here made. It will be no secret to those who know his writings that the commentaries on the individual paintings in this book were first drafted by Lionello Venturi.

F.K.

May 10, 1947

L.V.

UNDERSTANDING AND ENJOYING PAINTINGS

We recognize today that the very nature of art lies in creation—in the new life with which the individual artist endows his work of art.

Philosophy, through the centuries, has been very slow to apprehend that creation, that individual expression, is the essence of art, and the public has been still slower. The Greeks, thinking mainly of sculpture and painting, supposed that the essence of art lay in "imitation," as they called it—in the imitation of nature, or as we should say in representation. The merit would depend on the degree of *truth* to nature. This is a naive and recurrent belief, dominant again in the 19th century, and still very prevalent. We encounter it especially when dealing with the portrait, where fidelity or "likeness" is apt to seem, to the sitter, to his family and friends, and to others, as all-important, almost of sole importance. Such fidelity to nature could be minute conformity with the appearance of individual objects—what is called "naturalism" or "realism." It could also be fidelity to an imagined model beyond any individual work of nature—to an *ideal* of perfection. That is what is called "idealization."

This old popular conviction that merit in art resides in literalness of imitation of nature has had a rude shock, in modern times, through the invention of the camera. It is a little harder today than it used to be to hold this belief, now that a mechanical contrivance can exceed in such literal fidelity even the most gifted of human beings.

Meanwhile some of the greatest artists have realized instinctively that the essence of art must lie in something where man is much closer to the divine, where indeed, he approaches the divine most closely, in his power to create something new under the sun. As early as the Renaissance we find this thought hinted in scattered expressions of such supreme masters as Leonardo and Dürer. A clearer presentation of it was first made at the beginning of the 18th century by the philosopher Shaftesbury: "To copy what has gone before can be of no use. . . . To work originally, and in a manner create each time anew, must be a matter of pressing weight, and fitted to the strength and capacity of none but the choicest workmen." Like the true poet, the artist "is indeed a second maker, a just Prometheus, under Jove."

To create, one must give form, as the divine Creator did in forming the world from chaos. By giving form one creates a new entity, capable of its own continued existence, its own life. The best philosophers and poets alike have long recognized this. Schiller recognized it when he wrote "Art is living, breathing form." A molten unity must be impressed on the elements, whether those elements are drawn from the world around us, or from our own inner world of consciousness or dream. Fused in the crucible of the imagination, of the burning soul of the artist, the work of art emerges like a new crystal, with its own pattern of structure, its own novel perfection.

Woe be to him, unworthy of the name of artist, who tries merely to reproduce such a pattern, created by another. It has been the eternal hope of each generation to impose its own pattern and technique on the next, by a codification of artistic rules. That is what is meant by academism. There have been many academisms, and there will be many more, but all have failed and all will fail. The work of art cannot be created by any formula. In the attempt to apply one the fire will be lacking—no crystal at all will form. The true artist will not deign or need to use a formula; his own fire of creation will produce something vitally new and different.

Today the measure of our critical judgment is quite different from that of conformity to any rule. We put the accent on the personality of the artist, who goes beyond his own technical skill, his way of feeling and his theory of art, in order to create by his free imagination something new and personal which may appeal to our aesthetic interest and enjoyment. Any technique he uses and any ideal he follows are good if they are favorable to the free development of his imagination. There is no single technique good absolutely; it is good only in relation to the personality and imagination of the artist. The technique of Raphael is not better than that of Giotto. It is perfect for Raphael's art, as the technique of Giotto is perfect for his creations. Similarly, while the moral consciousness expressed by Rembrandt may be judged, from a purely moral point of view, as much superior to the languorous sensuousness of a Watteau, we realize that moral consciousness was necessary for the best creations of Rembrandt, languorous sensuousness was requisite for the masterpieces of Watteau. We do not think of Rembrandt when we enjoy Watteau, and vice versa. Thus we try to recreate the process of creation of the work of art, and evoke a corresponding enjoyment on our own part. We analyze the various components of it, in order to understand how the imagination of the artist created a whole which is not a sum of the components, but something new, where the whole personality of the artist reveals itself at once, in a work with its own unique perfection.

One of the consequences of modern methods of criticism is to widen the field of art, enabling us to appreciate and enjoy paintings belonging to any epoch and to any country, independently of the religion, the level of culture, the philosophy and the moral endeavor of the artist. Any image which is really created by imagination can be a work of art. On the other hand, we are aware that a painting is not a work of art whenever the painter submitted his imagination to activities of a different kind, when he passively obeyed fixed principles he had learned, or wanted to promote certain ideas, religious, social or moral, or fought polemically against others' opinions, or wanted to show his skill, or merely to make money—in short whenever he enslaved his imagination to interests foreign to it.

Of course, this does not mean that a high intelligence has no weight in the creation of a work of art, but the high intelligence of an artist shows itself by his knowing how to exclude from the work any interference of intellectual formulae, so that his imagination may be free to create. The same must be said for moral endeavor, which is necessary for the artist so that he can be true to his creative imagination and remain true to art, in spite of all the contingencies of life which distract his mind. We even know very well how in recent times some great artists had to face starvation in order to paint in a way which was despised by their contemporaries, and which later generations enjoyed and exalted.

The creation of an artist is connected with a world of experience; no artist ever created from nothing. An inspiration from nature has been and is still a good start for painting. This does not mean that the painter imitates nature, as many people still believe. Even photographers today know that to be artists they must introduce in their work something personal which does not depend on the imitation of nature. An inspiration from nature is an experience of our feeling and our imagination, and our experience is the condition of our creation of art.

When we paint a tree, which we have enjoyed looking at, we paint our own enjoyment of the tree. That is, the tree is only a stimulus to our enjoyment and a pretext for the representation of our enjoyment. This means that the real content of a work of art is something that belongs to the inner nature of man and not to the external nature of things. It is good for a painter to believe that he puts real things in his picture, as John Marin believes—good because this belief is a condition of the spontaneity of his transformation of things. But when we look at a watercolor by Marin we are aware that it is his transformation, or if you prefer, his style, which counts, and not the piece of nature recognizable in his picture.

Now we must recall that even the manner of enjoyment of a tree belongs to history. The way of looking at nature has changed very much through the centuries. A tree for Giotto and a tree for Marin are two completely different things. Without the Christian idea of a nature created by God, a tree by Giotto could not be as it is; and without that other historical event which is called Romanticism, a tree by Marin would be very different from what it is. The artistic quality of each of those trees does not consist in the fact that they are trees, but in the forms of the tree which the two painters created by impressing on them their mood, Christian or romantic. Thus the experience necessary for the creation of a work of art, even if it is the experience of a simple piece of external nature like a tree, is always conditioned by history.

A tree is one of the components of a picture. There are other subject matters: the choice of a Madonna by Giotto and the choice of a dancer by Renoir obey historical conditions in a broader way. The line of Giotto is related to the "Gothic" mode of visualizing, as the colors of Renoir are related to Impressionism. The plastic quality of Raphael belongs to the Renaissance style and the luminism of Rembrandt is the apex of Baroque composition. Extension on the surface or space in depth, gold or wall background, isolation of the image or its immersion in the atmosphere, relation between the image and its ambient, can be explained only by history.

A painter never represents anything without a process of choice and exclusion, in agreement with or in opposition to what he knows or feels about theoretical principles, religious or moral beliefs, and practical means. His choices and his exclusions reveal his taste. This word—taste—must not be confused with critical judgment. The latter affirms a truth, or what the critic believes is a truth; therefore it obeys an aesthetic theory, and its value finally depends on the value of the theory. But an artist does not always care for aesthetic theories; he may care only for his personal preferences, which favor his own work of art. If he succeeds in creating a work of art, his taste is good. If he does not succeed, we may truly say that his taste is bad. The taste of Raphael is good for Raphael and bad for any other artist, because nobody else had the particular kind of imagination which is Raphael's.

One may readily note that when artists of other periods, out of reverence for Raphael, introduced in their paintings certain elements of his taste, they lessened, instead of improving, their ability to create a work of art. Taste is an activity of man which is responsible for the choice he makes among the elements that his tradition, his epoch and his country offer him for the creation of art. Taste is thus the bridge between the personality of the artist and the civilization to which he belongs.

All this explains the choice of the hundred paintings we here offer the public in color plates. If we had considered only the strength of personality of the artists, we might have shown ten Rembrandts instead of three. But while our emphasis has been put on the personalities, we have also taken into consideration the various tastes they represent, to give an idea of what happened in the field of painting in Western civilization from the XIII to the XX century.

Taste in art and the taste of the artist have undergone many transformations. In the XIII century, painters did not want to study nature but to create symbols of the unseen—that is, of Divinity—by lines and colors. Then gradually the images became more individualized and represented a Divinity less detached from the experience of this world. The process was from the abstract to the concrete. Plastic quality became appreciated, imagination was more restrained than before. The gold background, symbol of Paradise, was replaced by the color of a wall. The mother of God became a dignified woman. Colors became subordinated to plastic form. Compositions and forms accepted a geometrical order and suggested a three-dimensional space behind the surface of the painting. For a while the images were isolated from their surroundings, because the interest of the painter was concentrated on the representation of man. Later on, however, interest grew in the relation between man and nature. The consequence was that plastic form could no longer suffice and that effects of light, which interpreted in one and the same way the image of man and the images of things, became predominant in painting. At the same time color was no longer subordinated to plastic form, but, by realizing the effects of light, again led the various components of painting.

The subject matter also changed. From the XIII to the XV century painters represented mainly divine images and sacred stories; later they showed their interest in man, his actions and his legends. At this time it was primarily the image of man which could express the feeling of the artist. But when the interest was extended to surrounding nature the feeling of the painter was expressed also by a wood, a river or a sky. Then new kinds of painting appeared, like landscape, and even still life, the representation of inanimate objects. When plastic form dominated, the physical body was shown first, and spiritual values were communicated through the bodies. But when effects of light absorbed the form of the bodies, the soul of things was revealed directly by the brush strokes. The relation between plastic form, on the one hand, and color and light on the other, changed again and again, now by a return to plastic form, now by a resuming of the experiences of color. Similarly the relation between imagination and sensibility changed, now by a predominance of imagination, illustrating human events, now by an expansion of sensibility, impressing a vibrating life on the most material elements of nature. When sensibility alone became responsible for the creation of art, and when the contemplation of appearances of color and light disregarded any notion of the objects of nature, painting was called impressionistic.

A reaction against Impressionism emphasized the rights of imagination and thought. Again the desire for abstract compositions of figures and the appreciation for decorative values detached painting from receptive sensibility. The study of nature was no longer the starting point for painting. The "absolute," that is, the abstractions of the mind, were preferred to the reactions of experience. Pure color meant color pure of the experience of reality; and it was harmonized by imagination. Abstract form meant form abstracted from the representation of things, and it became an ideal architecture. The process of creation was no longer from the concrete to the abstract, but again, as long ago, from the abstract to the concrete. Thus the process of creation of the painting reproduced in the first plate is like that in the last plate. The XIII century painter meets John Marin.

The circle is not closed; the development of taste is never ended. What happens in art is always unexpected, because it depends on the free imagination of men. Its variety, its continuous surprises, its human richness, are the source of the enjoyment to be found in the history of painting and in the plates of this book.

CONTENTS

ACKNOWLEDGMENTS

This work has been produced with generous cooperation and permission of the following museums and private collectors whose works are here reproduced.

ALBRIGHT ART GALLERY, BUFFALO · ART INSTITUTE OF CHICAGO, CHICAGO

JOHN NICHOLAS BROWN, NEWPORT · CARNEGIE INSTITUTE, PITTSBURGH

CHESTER DALE, NEW YORK · DETROIT INSTITUTE OF ARTS, DETROIT

FOGG MUSEUM OF ART, HARVARD UNIVERSITY, CAMBRIDGE

FRICK COLLECTION, NEW YORK · ISABELLA STEWART GARDNER MUSEUM, BOSTON

PHILIP L. GOODWIN, NEW YORK · A. CONGER GOODYEAR, NEW YORK

JOHN HERRON ART INSTITUTE, INDIANAPOLIS

HENRY E. HUNTINGTON LIBRARY AND ART GALLERY, SAN MARINO

JOHN G. JOHNSON COLLECTION, PHILADELPHIA · SAM A. LEWISON, NEW YORK

HENRY P. McILHENNY, PHILADELPHIA · METROPOLITAN MUSEUM OF ART, NEW YORK

MRS. G. MACCULLOCH MILLER, OLD WESTBURY, LONG ISLAND

MUSEUM OF FINE ARTS, BOSTON · MUSEUM OF MODERN ART, NEW YORK

NATIONAL GALLERY OF ART, WASHINGTON · WILLIAM S. PALEY, NEW YORK

PHILADELPHIA MUSEUM OF ART, PHILADELPHIA

PHILLIPS MEMORIAL GALLERY, WASHINGTON

YALE UNIVERSITY ART GALLERY, NEW HAVEN

Except in a few special instances, the original color plates were generously made available by the owners of the paintings. A large number were newly made especially for this book. The Frick Collection, through Frederick Mortimer Clapp, the Metropolitan Museum, through Horace H. F. Jayne, the Johnson Collection, through Henri Marceau, the Isabella Stewart Gardner Collection, through Morris Carter, the Phillips Memorial Gallery, through Duncan Phillips, were particularly liberal in making many of their masterpieces thus available to a broader public for the first time. The National Gallery of Art, through David E. Finley and Harry A. McBride, was likewise most cooperative, adding other masterpieces to those available in its own previous publications.

Plates 7, 29, 49, 60, 64, 67, 91, 92 were supplied by The Art Foundation, publishers of *Art News*, by courtesy of Alfred M. Frankfurter; plates 96, 98 and 101 by the Museum of Modern Art, by that of Monroe Wheeler; plate 81, by the publishers of *Life*; plate 100 by those of *Fortune*. Plates 53 and 66 were secured from Art Education, Inc.; plates 16, 20, 41, 55, 58 and 79, from Simon and Schuster, and plate 94 from Condé Nast Publications.

Owners of several paintings had them cleaned specifically to permit more adequate reproduction in this book. The making and proving of the original plates was under the oversight and approval of the owners, whether institutions or individuals. The plates were repeatedly corrected in comparison with the original works to insure fidelity.

The book was produced by the Beck Engraving Company under the intimate personal supervision of Charles W. Beck, Jr., who—in the volume *Masterpieces of the National Gallery of Art*—established the highest standards, here adopted. Its production of this book, including plates made at and for several different institutions by their own photoengravers, has presented even more difficult problems, which have been ingeniously solved by Mr. Beck to satisfy his own most fastidious requirements. All plates have been printed "one in line," generally with the very inks which were used in proofing the individual original plates. The layout was made, with equal fastidiousness, by Benjamin Collins, Art Director of the Beck Engraving Company. Their interest and skill are deeply appreciated.

GREAT PAINTINGS

IN AMERICA

1 · CENTRAL ITALIAN SCHOOL

XIII Century

ENTHRONED MADONNA AND CHILD

Panel. Height, 42 in.; width, 17½ in.

JOHN NICHOLAS BROWN, NEWPORT

(Lent to the Museum of Art, Rhode Island School of Design, Providence)

Among the many pictures of the XIII century representing the Madonna and Child enthroned, this one of the Brown collection must be considered of Central Italian origin because of its similarity to the Madonnas in Santa Maria in Via, Camerino, and in San Francesco, Mercatello, both in the Marches.

The fact that all the Madonnas of the XIII century can be grouped in three types has suggested that they obey conventions, even fixed laws of tradition, which did not allow the painters any individual interference, except for small details. If this opinion were to be accepted, when today we believe that any artistic value depends on the personality of the painter, we might deny that the paintings of the XIII century are works of art. But we feel that the contrary is true, and that, for example, the Brown Madonna is a masterpiece in painting. We must therefore reexamine the opinion on the conventionality of such painting, and understand what is the personal contribution of this anonymous painter.

The conventionality of the frontal position of the Madonna, and of the act of blessing of the Child is beyond any doubt. But both, position and act, belong to iconography—the study of what is represented—and not to the *art* of painting. The relation between the Madonna and the surface, the group and the throne, the way of realizing the framing of the Child by the body of the Madonna, the contours of the whole group, and the colors: all this is the individual visualization of the painter, and makes the painting unique among all those of the same time and place. And it is unique because it is the product of an individual imagination.

Here our understanding can be helped by what Theophilus wrote in the XII century. He suggested to the painters to stick to old models but to draw with an easy hand, and with faith in God, in order that their paintings could become spontaneously created. The authority of the old model descended directly from God, was revered as a revelation of God, but in the process of copying the painter modified this and that at his will. Small changes in the type, but a complete change in the visualization, transformed the copy into creation.

The background of the Brown Madonna is of silver, as is the throne. But between the images and the background is a curtain decorated by simple lines, tinted in red and blue. The same colors decorate the throne. Two different red tints color the cushion and the footstool. The Madonna is dressed in brown and red and has a white veil and a silver crown. The Child is dressed in brown and blue. Coloring is thus very simple, elementary; but the relation between the images and the curtain is dark and light, with an impressive pictorial effect, enhanced by the surrounding silver.

These contrasts in tone underline the abstract form of the image of the Madonna. The frontal type is not only the oldest one, but also the one best able to convey the severity of a divine image, its detachment from this world.

Italian painting of the XIII century has been and is rightly considered a branch of Byzantine painting. In the XIV century people were already aware that before Giotto the style in painting was "Greek," that is Byzantine. Plate 2 of this book illustrates a Byzantine painting, and it is easy to see the difference between the two Madonnas. The one in the plate 2 is extremely luxurious, as in the legends of the fabulous richness of the Near East. On the contrary the Brown Madonna, in spite of her crown and throne, is extremely severe and reserved. The mental structure of the image is close to that of a Romanesque country church.

The Brown painting is a simple Madonna and Child Enthroned belonging to familiar types, but it is also something else: the product of an individual visualization reflecting a state of mind which is proper to the XIII century in Italy. Religion and art, God and man, time and country concurred in the creation of a masterpiece.

16

2 · BYZANTINE SCHOOL

XIII Century

ENTHRONED MADONNA AND CHILD

Wood.   Height 33 in.; width 21 in.

Byzantine painting spread from the XII to the XIII century through all European countries.

The painting we illustrate was found in a convent in Calahorra, Aragon, Spain. There is nothing particularly Spanish in it. Some scholars have thought it was painted in Constantinople, others that it was painted in Sicily. This is mere guess work. The only certainty is that this is one of the best examples of painting of the XIII century in the Byzantine style.

It must be stressed that the Byzantine style is transcendental or supernatural in character. The painter wanted to represent beings in heaven. Thus he did not look about him at the people on this earth, but copied traditional models which he considered sacred images. The approximate resemblance of these images to human beings is the least important thing in the whole picture.

Of course an artist cannot create a work of art merely by copying models, or by supposing that the beings he represents are in heaven. His truly artistic activity begins after and beyond that. He must place his images on a surface and find a relationship between them. This is a problem of composition which can be solved only by the imagination of the painter.

In this painting we see the Madonna and Child with an accentuated vertical trend on a throne which creates a circular space around them. This space gives the images magnitude and dignity.

On the gold background are two circles, each containing a half figure of an angel, seen as though through a window of heaven. Their decorative value filling the space above the Madonna is evident. But beyond the decorative value is a mystic one. They appear: nobody knows whence or why; nobody knows what they are doing. They are justified only by the fancy of the artist, by his free imagining of an unknown world.

Isidor of Seville wrote in the VII century that beauty is something added to buildings for ornament and sumptuousness, such as golden roofs, or marble inlay, or multicolored paintings. During the Middle Ages this idea of beauty was predominant. The beauty of a painting consisted in the sumptuousness of its coloring. Thus the background is of gold, which is the most brilliant yellow in existence. To harmonize with the gold, colors must have the most intense brilliance, like precious stones or enamels. Hence the brilliance of red and blue in this painting. In later times the folds of garments were represented by chiaroscuro, that is the appearance of relief gained by the gradation of light and dark tones, irrespective of the colors used in producing them. Shadows, however, diminish the brilliancy of the colors. Thus the Byzantine painter represented the folds by radiating lines of gold: it was a symbolic representation, necessary to the color harmony. The neutral tones of the faces and of the throne are contrasting intervals, to enhance the most important parts of the heavenly vision, constituted by gold, red and blue.

The subject matter of this painting is a Madonna and Child, but the motif, which lends the artist his power, is a heavenly vision of dignity, luxury and sumptuousness.

3 · DUCCIO DI BUONINSEGNA

Siena, active 1278, died 1319

THE CALLING OF THE APOSTLES PETER AND ANDREW

Wood.   Height 16¾ in.; width 17¾ in.

KRESS COLLECTION. NATIONAL GALLERY OF ART, WASHINGTON

This painting was a part of a great "polyptych" which stood on the main altar of the Cathedral of Siena. A polyptych is a painting formed of many parts, each complete in itself. During the Middle Ages the richest cathedrals had altarpieces of gold and enamels. The Italians felt, however, that a painted scene could convey more human feeling than an enamel. Thus Duccio was commissioned to paint the cathedral altarpiece in 1308. When he finished it in 1311 tradition is that the whole population of Siena joyously accompanied the great work to its place. Now the major part of it is in the Museum of the Opera del Duomo in Siena. A very few parts, among them this one, are scattered outside Siena.

Duccio's style follows the Byzantine tradition, but his feeling calls for participation in the divine legend, as was the case in Gothic art, then just beginning to influence Italian painting. Duccio was little aware of this change, but, to express his feeling, he had, besides his transcendental vision, an ability to narrate, which is very winning.

He retains the gold background, which does not represent a sky but is a symbol of the light of Paradise. The poets of the time spoke of the radiant light of Paradise, which was so strong that no human eye could look at it. The figures have approximately natural shapes, but they, too, are symbols. Their action is not represented, it is suggested. What interests Duccio is the presentation of his figures. They are noble, dignified, reserved. They convey to the popular imagination their station, that is, their superior quality as Christ or as the Apostles. Their ranks are distinguished, the nobility of Christ being both moral and social, while that of Peter and Andrew, who belong to the workers' class, is only moral.

The rocks are sharply cut to emphasize their hardness, the water is treated softly to show its transparency and to reveal the fish in it. The net is punctuated to emphasize its distinguishing characteristic, the boat is strong to support the men. In this material field, also, the aim of the artist is thus not that of representing things naturally, but of symbolizing their qualities: of a rock, of a lake, of a net, of a boat. Hence the clearness and the appeal of the scene depend on the efficacy of each image as a symbol of its distinctive character.

The coloring is likewise symbolic. In nature colors are constantly changing under the influence of light and shade. Duccio cares very little for shadows, for chiaroscuro. What interests him is to find the tone which best reveals a characteristic. Gold is supreme for lustre. The rock is more yellow than any actual rock, but its yellow characterizes the rock with emphasis. The red, the blue, the sky-blue are good colors for the garments, the varied green is good for the water, the brown-black for the boat. They are enamel-like in order to harmonize with the gold. The composition is flat, on the surface. In this symbolic manner of painting the artist has no interest in three-dimensional effect.

Duccio did not abandon the general scheme of tradition. Within its limits he worked with deep penetration to humanize the sacred scene, and he succeeded in giving to the traditional forms an accent of charm and delicacy which goes beyond his own or any tradition, to become universal.

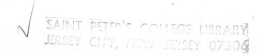

4 · SIMONE MARTINI

Siena, active 1315, died 1344

CRUCIFIX

Wood. Height 9¾ in.; width 5⅝ in.

This panel probably belonged also to a polyptych. Its elements are very few aside from the figure of Christ: a gold background, the summit of the hill of Golgotha, the cross with the label—Jesus of Nazareth, King of the Jews. The painting was an unimportant task, but small as it is, it is a masterpiece of art.

The figure is isolated, the background is the mere void from which the figure rises. By its neutrality and its extent this void helps to concentrate attention on the figure. The arms form a great inverted arch; the head, the chest, the legs, all hang downwards. The undulating lines of contours in the body as well as in the drapery, a few accents of light on the nose and on the blood spurting from the chest, reveal the creative imagination of the artist. They represent a poor martyr. An adorned halo is the symbol of the divine nature of that martyr. But such a symbol does not belong to art. It is the lines and the lights which express artistically His divine nature.

The image of a martyr evokes a feeling of pity, an affection for a victim of human cruelty. For many centuries Christ on the cross had been represented as a king, and the label at the top of the cross still recalls that He was a king. But Christian feeling does not consider the difference between a king and other men. It is for the man that the emotion of pity arises.

Nevertheless the crucified figure of Simone Martini is not that of a common man. One may say that Giotto's Madonna (No. 5) incarnates divinity in an average woman. In the figures of Simone, on the contrary, there is a refinement which suggests his interpretation of the divine as existing in the exclusiveness of a class, in the character of an aristocracy. This often narrows his ideal to the limits of a felicitous, subtle, delicate grace. Only when his imagination is confronted with drama is he able to go beyond the class limits of his ideal. He does so in this crucifix. The rhythm of lines emphasizes the slenderness of the victim and His suffering. At the same time the lines reveal His beauty, in spite of torment and death.

Simone Martini introduced into Sienese painting the Gothic line and its quality of refinement and delicacy. He understood also the emotional effect of that line. An eighteenth century writer, Della Valle, contrasted the Sienese with the Florentine school, as one of poets with one of philosophers. Today we should say that painters of both schools are poets but that the Florentines show more intellectual power, and the Sienese more mystical tenderness. Simone Martini certainly had less plastic energy than Giotto. But through his conventional lines he was able to realize his dreams of refinement and emotion to a degree which remained unsurpassed in his time, and perhaps in any time.

5 · GIOTTO

Colle di Vespignano (Florence), born about 1267, died 1337

MADONNA AND CHILD

Wood. Height 34⅝ in.; width 25 in.

In the painted altarpiece of which this painting was a part, it was the central panel. Three of the side wings have been found: a St. Stephen in the Horne Foundation, Florence, a St. John the Evangelist and a St. Lawrence in the André Collection, Châalis, France. Lorenzo Ghiberti mentioned a half figure of a Madonna with two other half figures at each side by Giotto in the Badia, Florence. It is possible this picture is identical with that one.

This Madonna belongs to the late period of Giotto, when he had lost something of his energy and had become more human and full of grace. The background is still of gold, as the church still wanted sumptuousness in altarpieces. The mediaeval ideal of beauty as richness of coloring has, however, been abandoned by Giotto. The blue mass of the Madonna's cloak is a dark one with folds obtained by gradations of shadow. The artistic function of the blue is not to conform to the gold by its brilliancy, but to contrast a shadowy mass with the brilliancy of the gold.

An entirely new function has been assumed by the uncovered parts of the flesh: faces, hands, a foot of the Child, His arms and His chest. Whereas in the Byzantine Madonna (No. 2) the painting of the flesh is the least interesting part of the whole, in Giotto's Madonna it is the most important. It is what gives character to the whole picture. In the Byzantine Madonna the ideal of the painter is realized by the brilliancy of color and by disregard for chiaroscuro; in Giotto's Madonna it is the chiaroscuro which achieves the plastic quality which is the formal ideal of the painter. The chiaroscuro discovers in the flesh-tints the best way of displaying itself, as these tints are light and detach themselves against the dark blue of the cloak. Thus the effect is double: the light flesh-tints against the dark cloak and the dark cloak against the light gold background. The latter belongs to tradition and is due to the demands of the Church of the Middle Ages. The former is the effect called for by the creative imagination of Giotto.

Giotto's plastic quality does not lend the images the full round appearance of a statue, but that of a basrelief. The appearance of a statue would be too material for Giotto. He is reserved, he does not want to take too great liberty with the image of a Madonna and Child. His religious feeling inspires him with respect and veneration. Hence the detachment of his images, and their participation in a divine life, which however is not separated from human life. It is the divine spirit which is incarnated in man.

Severe grace, dignity, monumentality are the aspects of these deified human images. They are the result of Giotto's plastic quality. Giotto's ideal is not realism. It is different from the Byzantine conception because of its plastic quality, but that is nonetheless an abstract, theoretical ideal. There are in Giotto's Madonna some realistic elements: the Child tries to take a rose, and grasps a finger of His mother in order to insure His stability. But these are details which do not change the ideal effect of the whole.

Giotto's power of uniting the divine and the human is the root of his importance in the history of art. At the beginning of the XIV century he proclaims that a new civilization is dawning, which will center its attention more and more on what belongs to man.

6 · PIETRO LORENZETTI

Siena, active 1320, died 1348

MADONNA AND CHILD WITH A MONK

Wood.   Height 49⅝ in.; width 29¾ in.

JOHNSON COLLECTION. PHILADELPHIA MUSEUM OF ART, PHILADELPHIA

This Madonna is one of the masterpieces of Pietro Lorenzetti and embodies his mature style. It comes from the Chigi-Saracini collection in Siena and is the central part of a polyptych. In the Hamilton collection, New York, were two angels which terminated the arch at the top of the picture.

In comparing Lorenzetti's Madonna with that by Giotto (No. 5), one becomes aware of profound differences between the styles of the two artists. These differences depend partly on the personality of the masters, partly on the moral climate of Siena, which is so remote from that of Florence.

Giotto's Madonna is shown as it would appear on a wall, hence its plastic effect. Lorenzetti's Madonna is shown as it would be seen within a room, at the moment when a monk kneels in adoration before the Child. The Child is full of anxiety at receiving the monk, the Madonna is sad over the future of her Child. Two angels look on. The subject matter is, like that of Giotto, a Madonna and Child, but the motif of the artist is entirely different. Lorenzetti does not display a sacred image but a scene of affection. Of course both Giotto and Lorenzetti, express their emotions— that is, their attitude towards the sacred legend. Lorenzetti not only expresses his way of feeling, but also the concrete feelings of his images. For him, feeling is related not only to the subjective artist but also to the objective image. The monk is not an image and not a portrait. It is an impulse to adoration, a stimulus of affection and humility, a pathetic dedication, to which the anxiety of the Child responds. The spiritual relationship between the Child and the monk constitutes the expressive center of the picture.

On the other hand, the Madonna shows a strong plasticity, an evident monumentality. We do not know if these qualities depend on the influence of Giotto, but it is probable. The hierarchical proportions (the largeness of the most important figure, the Madonna, and the smallness of the less important monk) depend on a tradition tending so to accentuate the dignity of the sacred image.

Thus we have a contrast between the expression of a human feeling, which belongs to this world, and the representation of an image, which belongs to heaven. This contrast is overcome by the Gothic line which has an artistic power in itself. Giotto does not emphasize the line, because he centers his attention on the plastic quality. But Lorenzetti needs a concentration of his plastic images on the relationship between the adoration of the monk and the anxiety of the Child. Thus the two images are compelled to move one towards the other; the mass of the Madonna, with the figures of the angels, must close and frame that movement. Hence the contour lines are emphasized, and by their undulating rhythm bring the plastic mass into relation with the expression of the feeling. In the work of Simone Martini line was often used for a decorative purpose. Lorenzetti's line is at once a function of plasticity and of movement, this latter being the physical aspect of the psychological effect. Hence unity of vision and expression is perfectly attained.

Lorenzetti's color is particularly complex. Following the tradition of Duccio and Simone Martini, he does not renounce the richness and delicacy of single colors. But he also wishes to use some colors as light and some as shadow, in order to correspond with the plastic effect. Hence a variety and a finesse of coloring which foretell the effects of a tonal style.

Together with his brother Ambrogio, Pietro Lorenzetti impressed his plastic style with varied and articulate forms and colors in order to heighten the expression of his feeling, even to the point of drama. This appealed to the popular feeling and was the basis of the wide influence he had on the Italian painting of the XIV century.

26

7 · BERNARDO DADDI

Florence, first mentioned 1312-1320, died about 1348

ST. CATHERINE BEFORE THE EMPEROR

Wood. Height 10¼ in.; width 13¾ in.

A predella, of which this small panel formed part, is the decoration of the base of an altarpiece. In the altarpiece proper, generally a polyptych, were the images of the Madonna and Saints; in the predella were depicted the events of their lives. Another part of the same predella, representing the Martyrdom of St. Catherine is also in the Metropolitan Museum, still another, representing St. Catherine in Prison is preserved in the Wauters Collection, Brussels.

Predellas offered to the Italian painters of the XIV and XV centuries an opportunity to develop their narrative qualities. The best of them, in their images, combined formal values in with imaginative values in order to achieve clarity. The representation of the event was conceived as a theatrical scene, with the simplicity and spontaneity proper to the old theatre.

The stage is formed by an open loggia, the wall being decorated by a rich brocade of a pattern influenced by the Near East. An emperor sits on his throne; the Saint, who is dignified by a crown and a halo, stands in front of him. Soldiers and civilians are looking on. The Saint appears isolated. With one hand on her heart she declares her Christian faith. It is an image of moral courage and simple grace. By raising an arm, with imperative command but without excitement. the emperor condemns her to martyrdom.

This is the simple story. The style is emphasized by the isolation of the Saint which endows her with strong plastic value, a higher relief than that of the other figures. It is this plasticity which establishes the center of vision as well as of the scene. To obtain it, representation of space is necessary. Without knowledge of scientific perspective the painter is able to suggest space by the lines of the loggia, by the transverse position of the figures around the Saint, and by the rhythm of light and dark colors.

Bernardo Daddi is one of the best of the followers of Giotto. He continues the latter's plastic trend, which achieves formal clarity, dignity, reserve, monumentality. But he does not refuse to hear from Siena the new voice of emotion and brilliancy of color. Above all the variety, richness and decorative effect of color differentiates Daddi from Giotto. He is less severe, less monumental, less powerful, but he has a new kind of grace and enchantment which is an artistic perfection in itself.

8 · SASSETTA

Siena, born 1392, died 1451

The Journey of the Magi

Wood.   Height 8½ in.; width 11⅝ in.

The Journey of the Magi was the upper part of an Adoration of the Magi the lower part of which has been recognized in a panel in the collection of Count Guido Chigi-Saracini at Siena. In the latter the Magi have arrived and actually offer their homage and their presents to the child Jesus. In our upper part, in the distance of the background, the painter narrates the fairy tale of the journey of the Magi and their picturesque court. Distance is a pretext for dream: Sassetta's fancy dreams with open eyes. This painting is one of the most popular in the United States.

Sassetta has many technical abilities. The bold foreshortening of a horse, the natural movement of the figures, the radiant light behind a hill, show that he is a good technician. But in this distant background of a painting he does not concern himself with plasticity, construction, and other ideals which he tries to reach elsewhere. Here he weaves in the purest way his narrative spell by characterising, one after another, all his figures. A mule is fatigued under its load, while a monkey rests comfortably, and the mule drivers beat their beasts with a stick. A small dog runs painfully, the head of the procession looks backward at its order, a cavalier peacefully holds his falcon, three pedestrians are weary of following the horses, the Magi with the halos of saints talk about God, and the servants about their earthly business. It is winter and it is dawn. In the subdued clarity of the day ducks fly in line, trees without foliage appear to have thorns, the earth is cut as if in a natural staircase, the star guiding the kings descends from heaven to earth. Many things are represented on such a very limited surface, yet the sense of solitude proper to winter envelops the cavalcade. The reason is that Sassetta devotes himself so fully, and so naïvely, to each image, that he impresses it with character and with spiritual isolation. It is not the ensemble, but the continuity of intense attention which creates the appeal. This is true of the forms as well as of the colors—as brilliant as gems, and isolated. It is a fairy tale for children. The hand is talented and mature but the soul is that of a dreamer. A rock quite as much as a face—everything is impressed by rapture for the vision of an enchanted world.

Sassetta is the best Sienese painter of the XV century at its beginning. He summarizes the refinement of the late Gothic tradition and the new popular feeling, the new adhesion to reality, which were characteristic of the early Renaissance.

9 · GIOVANNI DI PAOLO

Siena, active 1423-1482

MIRACLE OF ST. NICHOLAS OF TOLENTINO DURING A STORM AT SEA

Wood.   Height 20 in.; width 16 in.

JOHNSON COLLECTION. PHILADELPHIA MUSEUM OF ART, PHILADELPHIA

Of the polyptych to which this painting must have belonged, two parts survive: this panel and a St. Nicholas of Tolentino appearing above the Walls of a Town, in the Vienna Academy. It was painted in the period between 1455 and 1460.

Giotto's mosaic of the "Navicella" in St. Peter's in Rome, which became the most famous among his works and which today is so ruined that we can better know it through copies, was the model of almost all the representations of a storm at sea in Italian painting of the XIV and XV centuries. Giovanni di Paolo had in mind a model by Gentile da Fabriano, still depending on Giotto and representing the same scene of St. Nicholas, in a predella picture in the Vatican Gallery. He retained one feature from it, a swimming mermaid in the foreground. It was impossible for Giovanni di Paolo to repeat the scene of Gentile because of the different proportions of his panel, and he invented a composition of his own, one of those happy features which constitute his greatness.

The waves of the sea are solid cones like geometrical hills; it is the mermaid which reveals that they are waves. The ship is static; its ruin is indicated by the broken masts and by the desperate prayers of those on board. Behind a line which appears above the figures and the wave-hills, a calm, luminous sea begins. Against the dark sky five fragments of masts with their sails are born off by the furious wind. St. Nicholas of Tolentino appears to calm the sea and save the people.

Gentile da Fabriano had suggested the storm through a transverse composition, and had represented the transparency of water where the mermaid is swimming. He strove to depict the confusion of the sailors, who are trying to save the ship by throwing heavy cases into the sea, at the very moment when some of the crew become aware that St. Nicholas has appeared. This is naïve realism and gentle idealization.

The fancy of Giovanni di Paolo is totally different. The cones are symbols and do not represent the waves. The mermaid and certain light touches between the cones indicate that the cones are waves. The hull of the ship is so static that by itself it does not convey the idea of a storm. The facts are otherwise presented: the broken masts, the praying figures. The fine light surface of the calm sea is shown in the background without any representation of its distance. Thus it, too, is a symbol. The broken masts and the sails flying in the air have an elegance of line in which the fancy of the artist shows its greatest power, as well as a strange joy in unreality and destruction—a sadistic touch.

Giovanni di Paolo does not represent the miracle of St. Nicholas, he rather presents some symbols of the event. In other words, abstraction enters between the painter and the subject-matter in order to give a mysterious meaning to the most simple images. Thus in a naïve form Giovanni di Paolo forecasts the trend of mood which paved the way to surrealism.

10 · FRA ANGELICO

Vicchio di Mugello, born 1387, died 1455

CRUCIFIXION

Wood. Height 33⅞ in.; width 14¼ in.

FOGG MUSEUM OF ART, HARVARD UNIVERSITY, CAMBRIDGE

It was doubtless to serve the piety of a private person, probably a monk, that this panel was painted. Perhaps it belonged to a diptych, or pair of paintings; certainly it was put on an altar in a private room as an incentive to prayer. This use is a condition of the artistic achievement. Compare the work with the crucifix by Simone Martini (No. 4). Simone's piety was concentrated on the drama of Christ, his suffering and the cruelty of man. The feeling of Fra Angelico is entirely different. His Crucifixion is a ceremony around Christ on the cross, a beautiful figure, dignified, and very well composed. The pity arises from symbols such as the cross, the nails, the crown of thorns, the blood from the wounds. But the beauty of form calms and veils the drama. The same thing may be said of the figures of Mary and St. John the Evangelist. They participate in the drama, they pity and weep, but their gestures are so designed as to create beautiful figures. The monk has been identified as Juan de Torquemada, a Dominican, who was made a cardinal in 1439, and is known for his doctrines in theology and law. Fra Angelico painted him as a naïve little figure who, in a graceful pose, adores an image of God.

Fra Angelico was a very pious man. He painted during his whole life with the single purpose of serving and exalting God. When in the XIX century the Christian quality of art again became appreciated and the Italian primitives were admired, Fra Angelico was considered by Rio the best representative of the mystic school. No doubt Fra Angelico was a mystic. But between the drama of Golgotha and his mystic feeling, his way passed through a preoccupation with the dignity of the church and through a desire for beauty. His participation in the old sacred drama was less direct than that of Simone Martini. His images became actors in the presentation of a drama—marvelously sensitive actors, to be sure. Those who consider beauty to be the unique ideal of art, will prefer Angelico to Simone, and Raphael to Angelico. But those who appreciate in art freedom of imagination and intensity of feeling will see in Simone Martini a higher humanity and a greater power of universality.

Fra Angelico was almost the contemporary of the greatest founders of the humanistic style. He was fourteen years older than Masaccio. Because of his religious feeling and surroundings he remained more faithful to tradition in art than did the Humanists. At the same time, however, he assimilated the principles of plastic quality and formal beauty which the Humanists sponsored. Thus he found a balance between religious expression and worldly beauty which is unique, and which explains the widespread enthusiasm for his paintings. He uses undulating lines only for the contours of plastic figures, hence their dignity. The colors are as brilliant as precious stones; they have a minimum amount of chiaroscuro necessary for plasticity. Fra Angelico was a felicitous technician, he could easily do what he liked. Hence his ability and his ready power of assimilation. But he also felt it necessary to restrain himself from adopting the daring novelties of his time in order to express his veneration both for sacred legend and for artistic tradition. The gold background, the brilliant colors, the isolation of figures, the presentation of images preferred to the representation of a scene, all this belongs to tradition. But the plasticity and the monumentality of the group constitute the novelty. At the top, the tree with the symbolic pelican, fabled to feed his young with his own blood, is a touch of fancy full of appeal.

In the transition between the end of the Middle Ages and the dawn of the Renaissance Fra Angelico was fortunate enough to combine the best of two civilizations. And his application of the mystical impulse to the gracious walls of his convent was his own path to the humanization of the divine.

11 · MASOLINO

Panicale (Florence), born 1383, last recorded 1435

THE ANNUNCIATION

Wood.   Height 58¼ in.; width 45¼ in.

Humanist painters were not contented with the presentation of plastic images, they wanted to create by perspective the proper space wherein to show their figures. The gold background, with its transcendental implications, was abandoned and replaced by an interior. In order to indulge in bright coloring and to avoid the interference of the shadows usual in an interior, the room has been conceived as an open loggia. Its depth in space is shown by a vault and an open door towards other rooms in the background.

Masolino's aim however is not to insist on the construction of space, he wishes, rather, to adorn it. He decorates almost everything—from the walls, the ceiling, the vault and the door, to the garments of the Angel Gabriel. This balance between construction and decoration is at once expert and naïve, and thus is very charming. In the drapery of the Madonna the undulating lines are the tribute paid by the painter to the taste of the international late Gothic. The plastic quality of the bodies and above all of the faces, however, belongs to the new humanistic taste of which Masaccio is the great representative in painting. Like Fra Angelico, Masolino does not want to break with tradition, but he has not the religious impulse of Angelico. His only deity is grace.

This grace is the result of proportion and variety in the elements of architecture, in their multicolored brightness, and in the delicacy of the nuances of light. Shadows are excluded as much as possible. Only the bright aspect of the world is shown, which is delightful and shows a youthful timidity in the painter. However the vault is dark, and the ensemble of the figures, also, appears as dark against light. The open door has a special charm because the play of light becomes complex, being illuminated both from the foreground and from the background. The inlaid wood of the door and the fabric of the curtain react to light in different ways. This is richness of pictorial quality; it is vitality in painting, and is grace.

Another and stronger, if not better, accent of grace is laid upon the heads and hands. They seem as if formed of a fairy-like marble, whiter and more delicate than the finest Parian marble, to conform with the very blond hair. Ecstasy through the grace of youth has very seldom been so absolute and so complete. The splendor of color, fresh and pure, surrounds that grace with a magic halo.

Grace is a beauty of divine origin. One may speak of physical beauty, not of physical grace. Thus beauty must receive a spiritual touch to become grace. True religious inspiration enabled Fra Angelico to create many images of grace. Masolino was not religiously inspired when he was painting. What he longed for was to create an object of beauty in the humanistic sense. His character, however, was too sweet and respectful fully to incorporate the humanistic revolution. Mediaeval tradition, the religious subject matter, the purpose of the painting, which was to be placed upon the altar of a church—all this maintained in the picture a spiritual inspiration which is responsible for its grace.

12 · FRA FILIPPO LIPPI

Florence, born about 1406, died 1469

MADONNA AND CHILD

Wood.   Height 31⅜ in.; width 13⅛ in.

After having been in the Solly collection, London, until 1821, the painting passed to the Prussian state and was formerly in the Kaiser Friedrich Museum, Berlin. It came to the National Gallery of Art as part of the Kress Collection in 1939.

The humanistic style has reached its maturity in this picture. The gold background is excluded, the ornamental niche constitutes an architectural space to which the figures are related. The plastic ideal dominates all other artistic elements.

In 1428, after the death of Masaccio, who had revived the plastic ideal, certain artists, such as Fra Angelico and Masolino, remained in Florence. They had learned from Masaccio how to achieve plasticity, but they were perhaps not young enough to follow his ideal to its ultimate conclusion. Fra Filippo Lippi, on the contrary, was younger than Masaccio. He soon became one of the best representatives of the new trend, which detached painting from the tradition, under religious predominance, of the Middle Ages. Fra Filippo was a monk, but not so good a monk as he was a painter. Documents confirm the legend that he managed to help a nun escape from her convent, that he was pardoned by the pope because he was a good painter, and that she had a child by him, Filippino Lippi, who became a good painter too. This sensual temperament of Fra Filippo is thoroughly confirmed by his pictures. The power of the plastic bodies is overwhelming. In the material roundness of forms Filippo attains the personal character of his art. He remained a pious man, and the faces of his figures express sweetness, kindness and modesty, revealing his reverent attitude toward the divine images he painted. But his temperament was too strong to conceal his enthusiasm for the flesh.

Masaccio had a moral conscience, which permitted him to impress his plastic images with a high religious feeling. Fra Filippo's conscience was not equally strong. Thus his accent was on material plasticity. On the other hand, his sensual tendency was favorable to art. He was, in fact, the first painter definitely to break with Gothic tradition, and to manifest the new trend with coherence and consistency. The group of the Madonna in this picture is a good example of this. The folds are large and deep and strong, as if of rock. This results from the sincerity of his plastic expression. A very happy achievement is the head of the infant Jesus. The hands also are likewise beautifully molded.

A consequence of the contrast between Fra Filippo's sensuous plasticity and his ideal is apparent in his coloring. The Middle Ages, with its dream of precious colors, is gone, and with it the chromatic refinement of the Gothic style. Fra Filippo subordinated his coloring to chiaroscuro and to plastic effect. He is a virtuoso in coloring, to be sure. Virtuosity, however, is a matter of technique. He knows how to manage color, but he does not feel ecstasy for a harmony of colors. Yet from this, likewise, which may be considered a defect, arises an advantage for art. Effects of chiaroscuro do not need color, and plasticity is pure when colors are subdued. The faith Fra Filippo had in plasticity was sufficient to transform all his shortcomings into artistic merits. This could only be true because he was a genius.

He had many followers, the greatest of all being Botticelli.

13 · DOMENICO VENEZIANO

Active in Florence. First recorded 1438; died 1461

SAINT JOHN IN THE DESERT

Wood.   Height 11¼ in.; width 12½ in.

KRESS COLLECTION. NATIONAL GALLERY OF ART, WASHINGTON

This painting belonged to the predella of an altarpiece painted for the church of Santa Lucia de' Magnoli in Florence, which is now in the Uffizi Gallery of that city. The other parts of the predella are scattered through various museums, the National Gallery, Washington, the Fitzwilliam Museum, Cambridge, the Berlin Museum.

The youthful St. John the Baptist is shown at the moment when he is discarding his clothes in order to wear an animal skin. All around is desert, mountainous rocks with sparse bushes. That desert, however, is not imagined as fearful, suggesting pity for the young boy. It is too beautiful for that. Even though hard, it is vibrating and monumental.

Domenico Veneziano has at his disposal all the means necessary to represent nature naturally, but his fancy still successfully dominates the depiction. The nude correctly drawn, the mass of rocks made sharply evident by the effect of light, the blue sky and the white clouds do not interfere with the character of the whole as a fairy tale. It is essential to the picture that the rocks are pointed, that their transverse lines suggest a sort of movement, like the appearance of reality to an imagination which modifies it and emphasizes the human re- action to it.

All this is heightened by the coloring, which reveals a new experience of the artist in observing the rela- tionship between light and color. In order to emphasize this experience, Domenico Veneziano uses a double tone in every local color. To begin with, he frames his painting with a border of two tones of pink. The cliffs are of two greys, the trees and bushes of two greens, the water of two light blues, the sky of white-blue and blue, the skin of two browns, the dress of two reds, the tunic on the ground of white and grey. The flesh tints are grey and the hair is brown. The foreshortened halo is a touch of real gold bordered with red. These dou- ble tones thus suggest the illuminated and the shadowy side of each object. Hence the richness of coloring, even when the tint is neutral. It is light which gives a character of color even to the grey, and gives a sense of reality even to the most fantastic forms. The work is a masterpiece of painting as well as of poetry.

Domenico Veneziano was born in Venice and must have received his first education in the late Gothic style of North Italy, where the dominant tradition was one of color, but without effect of light and shade. We know of Domenico's activity, however, only after he participated in Florentine art. He absorbed from Floren- tine art the sense for three-dimensional space and its rendering through perspective, the plastic drawing of human figures, the conception of painting within the limits of human experience.

It was the impact of the Florentine tradition of plastic form on his tradition of Gothic coloring which in- spired Domenico Veneziano to create a visual medium which could harmonize both. Chiaroscuro is based on the gradation from white and black, neither of them being considered colors. When a painter uses a colored tone to represent light and another colored tone for shade, he goes beyond chiaroscuro, into the pictorial rep- resentation of light and shade. This was what Domenico created for the first time in Florence, and his crea- tion, developed by his pupil Piero della Francesco, influenced the whole course of Italian painting.

Instead of developing his new creation, Domenico contemplated it with a naïve eye, with the spontaneity and frailty proper to any new beginning. Hence his incomparable charm, and the character of a fairy tale which anything acquires under his brush.

14 · PIERO DELLA FRANCESCA

Borgo San Sepolcro, born c. 1410, died 1492

SAINT JOHN THE EVANGELIST

Wood. Height 51¹³⁄₁₆ in.; width 22¾ in.

FRICK COLLECTION, NEW YORK

This painting, probably representing Saint John the Evangelist, is part of an altarpiece which has been identified with the one ordered of Piero della Francesca by the Chapter of the Church of Saint Augustine, Borgo San Sepolcro, in 1454. The painting was finished in 1469. Two other parts of the same altarpiece are known: St. Nicholas of Tolentino in the Poldi-Pezzoli Museum in Milan, and St. Michael the Archangel in the National Gallery, London.

In the lower left-hand corner of the Frick panel there appears a block of brownish marble which covers part of the saint's right foot. Some lines remain of a second block. The two blocks are the base of a Madonna's throne, as Mr. Millard Meiss has demonstrated: thus the central panel represented the Madonna enthroned; Saint John and St. Michael were immediately at the sides of the Madonna.

The Frick painting is one of the greatest masterpieces of Italian art. It presents many aspects for us to consider. Three aspects however must be emphasized: the powerful plastic mass, the particular kind of coloring, and the moral implications of these.

In Fra Filippo's Madonna (No. 12) there is also a powerful plastic mass, but that of Piero della Francesca is quite different. It is even more powerful, but its chiaroscuro is less insistent, has less weight; it does not seem like a rock. It is less sculptural and more pictorial; its lightness has a spiritual value. Piero della Francesca is a master of perspective and even a theorist regarding it; but his aim is to present a figure constituting a mass occupying space, not to represent an action, even the simple one of being seated. Thus to discover his interest in perspective one must look at the details like the steps of the throne or the open book or the feet, which are resting on the ground. These are solidly posed, not for their weight, but for their foreshortening. As for the whole figure, the plastic mass is due to the contrast of colors more than to chiaroscuro: the red of the mantle against the yellowish-white of the parapet and the blue of the sky, also the white of the hair and the beard against the brown of the face. The result is that the plastic masses are more detached than relieved; the work is more pictorial than sculptural.

Piero della Francesca thus has the new conception of color, which we have seen in Domenico Veneziano. While Fra Filippo sacrificed color to obtain a plastic quality, it is through color that Piero della Francesca obtains his plastic quality. While chiaroscuro is conceived as the relationship of white, gray and black apart from colors, Piero della Francesca uses one color for light and another color for dark, thus creating through color an effect of light and shade, which is richer, more varied and broader than chiaroscuro. In other words, it is color which creates plastic form. To understand the novelty of this way of coloring one must look at Fra Angelico (No. 10) or Masolino (No. 11): these painters followed the Gothic tradition of coloring, most delightful and graceful. But Piero della Francesca's coloring has a new depth, a new impact, a new coherence. Color is the structure of the whole painting. This new function of color influences its quality; the red is not only a beautiful red, it is a living whole, a creation in itself, a window open on a dream. The same must be said of the white and the brown.

The effects of light and shade need movement in order to reveal the cosmic vibration of the rays. But this aspect of light is renounced by Piero della Francesca. He dreams of regular forms, and emphasizes in forms what is closest to abstract geometry. Nothing is more static than a geometrical figure. Thus the vibration of his light is crystallized, and assumes the aspect of eternal stability, accentuating the solidity and monumentability of his figures.

Therefore it is difficult to say which was greater in him, his power of realization or his impulse toward abstraction. In logic a contradiction must be resolved by a synthesis. But in art a contradiction may survive in a balance where contrasting elements exalt each other.

None of the pictures reproduced in the previous plates has such power of evoking reality and life as has this image. At the same time a desire for contemplation goes beyond that life and creates an image of dignity, of concentration in learning, which is alive today as it was when created—an image at the highest level of humanity.

15 · ANDREA DEL CASTAGNO

San Martino a Corella (Dicomano, Tuscany) born 1423, died 1457

DAVID

Leather. Height 45 in., width 32 in. above, 17 in. below

WIDENER COLLECTION. NATIONAL GALLERY OF ART, WASHINGTON

This work decorates a leather parade shield. It represents David, who was a symbol of the freedom and independence of the Florentine people.

The activity of Andrea del Castagno, who died very young, must be limited to between 1440 and 1457. He assimilated some of the new principles in painting brought forward by Domenico Veneziano and Piero della Francesca, and he felt with the dramatic power of the Florentine sculptor Donatello. This David is one of the most beautiful and less dramatic among the works of Castagno. Still if one compares it to the Saint by Piero della Francesca (No. 14), one is aware of the moral excitement which is proper to Castagno. Look at the sky: instead of the diaphanous blue there is a dark blue interrupted by numerous clouds. It is true that these clouds are small and modest; we are accustomed to fearsome, big clouds in romantic painting. But it is also true that Castagno's little clouds have accents of movement and energy, and suggestions of surrealistic forms.

The image of David is presented on the surface, with a supreme elegance of forms, of balance and rhythm. It is not only a presented image, however, it is in action. The severed head of Goliath is at his feet. He still holds his sling and turns towards his people, raising his left hand to announce his victory. The echo of the struggle just finished reverberates in his hair, which seems full of snakes, the fatigued features of his face, the short clothes fluttering in the wind, and the sharp contrasts of light and shade of the rocks. The ideal of beautiful forms does not allow Castagno to abandon himself to a dramatic movement, but he creates a contemplation of movement.

The color is as deep and structural as that of Piero della Francesca. But a new element has been introduced: line. It is a line which has a value both for itself and as a function of plastic qualities. It conditions the whole image and its movement, and creates the beauty of the legs and arms. It is this line which, while revealing the movement, gives the image a highly intellectual value, the poetical quality of contemplation.

Like his best contemporaries, Andrea del Castagno knows how to bear full witness to reality, but at the same time he goes beyond reality and enters into a dream world where imagination creates an ideal of human power. The image he has created dominates rocks and clouds, as well as the evil spirit. It stands for the triumph of youth, with its mixture of physical strength and naïve goodness.

44

16 · ANTONIO POLLAIUOLO

Florence, born about 1432, died 1498

THE RAPE OF DEJANIRA

Wood (now canvas). Height 21⅜ in.; width 31¾ in.

JARVES COLLECTION. YALE UNIVERSITY ART GALLERY, NEW HAVEN

Humanistic culture drew the attention of painters and amateurs to mythological legend. Religious feeling had given the proper content to the majority of works of art during the Middle Ages. Greek mythology, however, could not arouse religious feeling in Florence during the XV century. The subject matter of this picture is The Rape of Dejanira, but Pollaiuolo was not able to take the legend seriously; his real content had to be something else.

The Middle Ages had accentuated the transcendance of religion, and the importance of heaven as opposed to that of earth. Humanistic culture with its paganism was concerned above all with this earth. The mythological legend of Hercules was a pretext for showing the energy and agility of man through anatomy, and the liveliness of a landscape through perspective. From the beginning of the XV century in Florence geometrical perspective was known to painters; as for anatomy, Antonio Pollaiuolo was interested in it more than any one else. His aim in using anatomy was not science but art; it was the energy and the pleasure of a well constructed body that the painter had in view. The figure of Hercules is a masterpiece of contemplation of movement, rather than the representation of a real action. With such a purpose line is not limited to the contours, but continues within the bodies and finds its own rhythm. The action of Hercules shooting an arrow across a stream, of the centaur Nessus holding the captive Dejanira, of the woman's trying to escape, is presented in its essence rather than represented as a real action. In homage to feminine beauty the painter stressed certain abstract geometric elements, such as the oval of the face, the cylinder of the arms, unaware that these geometric elements are obstacles to any movement. It is because of this that the movement of Hercules and the centaur appears much more natural than that of Dejanira.

However, in his search for energy and movement, Pollaiuolo did not limit himself to the use of lines and anatomy. The river which Nessus is crossing moves rapidly, and its water is foaming. This movement cannot be rendered by lines, but only by touches of light shining through a mass of shadows. The same thing may be said of his landscape which, in spite of its linear perspective, comes to life in a succession of dark and light tones.

The dignity of man, the centering in man of the whole of nature, becomes insecure in Pollaiuolo's art. He is only interested in depicting man's struggle in life, forcing the whole of nature to participate in his struggle. The link between nature and man is closer in Pollaiuolo's vision than in that of any of the previous Florentine artists. This link is movement, a quality that belongs to both nature and man.

The center of Pollaiuolo's picture is no longer man but the river, and, in spite of their occupying the foreground, the drama of the three figures becomes only an episode. We can hardly say that the painter wanted merely to include his figures in the landscape. What he did was to juxtapose figures and landscape, the unity of that juxtaposition consisting in the quality of movement. It was this quality that Pollaiuolo represented, rather than the story of Hercules and Dejanira. Thus he was able to go beyond his representation of reality, however powerful, to attain the ideal values of energy and vibration.

17 · SANDRO BOTTICELLI

Florence, born 1444-5, died 1510

THE MADONNA OF THE EUCHARIST

Wood.   Height 33 in.; width 24¾ in.

By drawing the attention of the artist to the world where we live, humanistic culture translated into moral values the traditional religious requirements. Botticelli had acquired from Fra Filippo and Pollaiuolo the new humanistic science of painting, that is perspective, anatomy, chiaroscuro and plasticity. His soul however was deeply religious, as is proved not only by his work but also by his adherence, in his later years, to the movement led by Savonarola. At the same time he was deeply interested in the profane world of classic literature. His painting is perhaps the outstanding sign of this opposition between the new culture and the ancestral faith, which constituted a conflict in the whole course of the Italian Renaissance.

The Madonna of the Eucharist is an early work of Botticelli. He has just overcome his dependence on Fra Filippo and Pollaiuolo and created a completely personal style. In the very moment of its creation, this style has a rare freshness and a spontaneity.

This painting was not conceived as an altarpiece, even though it once adorned a private altar. It is a familiar scene within a closed space: a mother, a child and a young man of the same family. Their infinite grace and their natural dignity are qualities which may likewise be found in the secular as well as in the religious world. All three figures, however, are intent of a religious rite. The young man, who is an angel, is offering a dish of grapes and ears of corn as a symbol of the Eucharist. The Madonna takes an ear of corn, the Child blesses it. They are human beings meditating on a religious mystery.

The plastic forms, which are very strong, large and sure, testify to their figures being human—to their concrete reality. It is a plastic reality less sharp, but even greater and more developed than that of Fra Filippo Lippi (No. 12). A new source of artistic life modifies the plasticity: it is line. Botticelli inherited this from Pollaiuolo, but he thoroughly transformed it. Botticelli's line does not aim at stressing energy and movement. It has a rhythm in itself, which conditions and unifies the composition, contours the forms, determines the poses, and accompanies the folds of the garments. There is a continuous undulation, determined on the surface by line, and also developed in depth through chiaroscuro. In the three faces it is clear that chiaroscuro, while realizing the human form, obeys an intimate rhythm of gentle rise and fall. This rhythm is the spiritual touch of the whole painting. It corresponds to an ideal, and it represents no other thing.

When we speak of undulating line we readily recall the Gothic style which was based especially on the effects of line. What distinguishes Botticelli is the extensions to the planes of this rhythm of the line. He has been called the "greatest poet of line." There are many "poets of line," even many great ones. We can readily understand this enthusiasm for Botticelli's line, however, because it is very subtle and delicate, and because one cannot specify where the line ends and the plasticity begins. This factor of transmutation is the real source of Botticelli's grace.

It was not accidental, however, that he again took up an artistic element which had had such great success in the Middle Ages. There is a correspondence between the undulating rhythm of Botticelli and his religious feeling. That rhythm was a way of connecting the new culture of the Humanists with the old faith of the Middle Ages.

18 · SANDRO BOTTICELLI

Florence, born 1444-5, died 1510

THE ADORATION OF THE MAGI

Wood.   Height 27¼ in.; width 40⅝ in.

This painting was famous when it still belonged to the Hermitage in Leningrad. It is now one of the leading masterpieces of painting in the United States. It belongs to Botticelli's Roman period (1481-1482), when he painted in the Sistine Chapel of the Vatican and engaged for the first time on large undertakings in fresco.

Its composition is a perspective one: not only is the ruined building calculated along perspective lines, but so above all are the positions of the figures. Two groups of horses and horsemen of the court of the Kings closes the horizon of the foreground. Far distant in the landscape is another horizon. The center of the whole is the Madonna and Child, a very slender group, modest, delicate and gentle. It was intentional on the part of Botticelli to put in motion the many men, old and young, richly clothed, to bow before a poor child. This is the meaning of the whole scene, a purely Christian meaning. The strength and energy of the painting are concentrated in the men and their passion; their varying attitudes and expressions are powerful. In this lies the artistic power of the painter; here he expresses his interest in life. It is he who bows to the Christian myth, after having evoked all the potentates of the earth. His devotion is so intense that he does not fall into rhetoric; it is not only his sincere faith, it is also his artistic power which prevents hypocrisy. In fact the contrasts of the attitudes and the expressions of the men reach a dramatic value beyond the content of the scene. It is the power of a visionary who loves the expression of action not for action itself, but for expression. Here we can understand how even drama must be lyrical to reach pure art.

This lyricism is objectified in lines and colors. The rhythm of lines is obvious, as it conditions everything. One point to be stressed, however, is that the perspective space contrasts with the lines as well as with the movement brought forth by the lines. Botticelli knows perspective space and profits by it, but he is intolerant of its limitations. He is too free, too visionary, to obey any rule, too spiritually moved to be satisfied with the statics of perspective space. No doubt he feels a sort of uneasiness before the humanistic faith in man and he escapes from it in a romantic feeling for an outer world.

So far as Botticelli's color is concerned, one must remember his early dependence on Fra Filippo Lippi and the latter's system of subordinating color to plastic form. Thus Botticelli never adopted the use of color as light and shade, as did Domenico Veneziano, Piero della Francesca and also Pollaiuolo. He had a natural sensibility for coloring, however, and he transformed chiaroscuro in a fanciful chromatic gradation of contrasted light and dark zones, or exalted some precious single colors. The Adoration of the Magi is one of the masterpieces of Botticelli's coloring, above all in the two groups of men. One must admit, however, that his chromatic value exists more in the details than in the whole.

The building is in ruins. Botticelli wanted to suggest a classical temple, but his architecture is in the style of the Renaissance. In other pictures, also, he liked to represent ruins, not for the poetry of ruin, but for the interruption they make in regular forms—another sign of the restlessness of his spirit.

His landscape has no value in itself; is only a pretext for a broad space and a distant horizon against a peaceful, light sky. In the distance of the landscape his spirit rests.

19 · ANDREA MANTEGNA

Isola di Carturo, born 1431, died 1506

THE ADORATION OF THE SHEPHERDS

Wood (now canvas).   Height 15¾ in.; width 21⅞ in.

METROPOLITAN MUSEUM OF ART, NEW YORK

The culture of Humanism, which originated in Florence, reached Padua and Venice somewhat later. Andrea Mantegna, who was educated in Padua and worked there and in Mantua, was the founder of humanistic painting in the whole of North Italy. Perspective, anatomy, drawing, even more than chiaroscuro, were the ideals of Mantegna. He strove to realize them with so formidable an impulse that he attained, from his early youth, a perfection of his own.

Our painting perhaps belonged to the predella of a large altarpiece. It was executed about 1460, in Mantegna's early period. His style, however, is fully mature. Perspective is emphasized not only in the landscape but also in the position of the figures. The figures are represented in attitudes which have an importance in themselves, attitudes which are self-contained and are not subordinated to the significance of the action. A typical example is that of the shepherds, who turn to adore the sleeping St. Joseph rather than Christ, which is incongruous with the significance of the scene. It is this incongruity, however, which illuminates the nature of the painter. No doubt the shepherds are symmetrical with the figure of St. Joseph: to emphasize perspective symmetry, Mantegna neglects suitability of representation. Moreover between the figures of St. Joseph and the shepherds there is a spacial void which induces an ecstasy of anticipation. The painter seeks to obey his severe rule and draws from it a hint of mystery. The line which unites the St. Joseph, the head of the Madonna and the back of the first shepherd forms an arch, suggesting the architectural character of the vision. But within the architectural composition, Mantegna stresses the details in order to emphasize the reality of his images.

The folds of the costumes are portrayed with the utmost accuracy. The forms of the bodies and faces are so insistent that, at least in the case of the first shepherd, they become brutal and distorted. His torn hose are emphasized to such a degree that the fabric assumes the solidity of metal. The stones are cut into so many small parts and with such precision that it seems as though the painter would like to extend the idea of anatomy from the human body to the rocks. The orange tree in the foreground and all the details of the landscape, in addition to the two peasants approaching from the middle ground at the right, who form an attractive genre scene, are painted with realistic accuracy. Noteworthy, also, is the intimate and charming scene of the cherubs around the child Jesus. This realism and this intimate poetry are not connected with the classical ideal of the Humanists. The architectural ideal of the composition is humanistic, as well as the structural character of the drawing. But the concentration on details is, on the contrary, of Gothic character. Mantegna's coloring is also still Gothic. He is too fond of colors to sacrifice them to chiaroscuro, and he obtains the plasticity more through repeated lines than through chiaroscuro. Nor does he harmonize colors with light and shade as does Piero della Francesca. His coloring is above all decorative, and aims at rendering the preciousness of every image.

The classical ideal was only a frame for Mantegna's art. He drew from it a high intellectual rank and a moral consciousness. The very essence of his genius, however, was the deliberate insistence on the lines, on the details and on the preciousness of colors, thus to vitalize everything he touched with his brush. The contrast between these two trends, the architectural abstraction and the detailed concreteness, gave way to a mood of mystery which attained magical power.

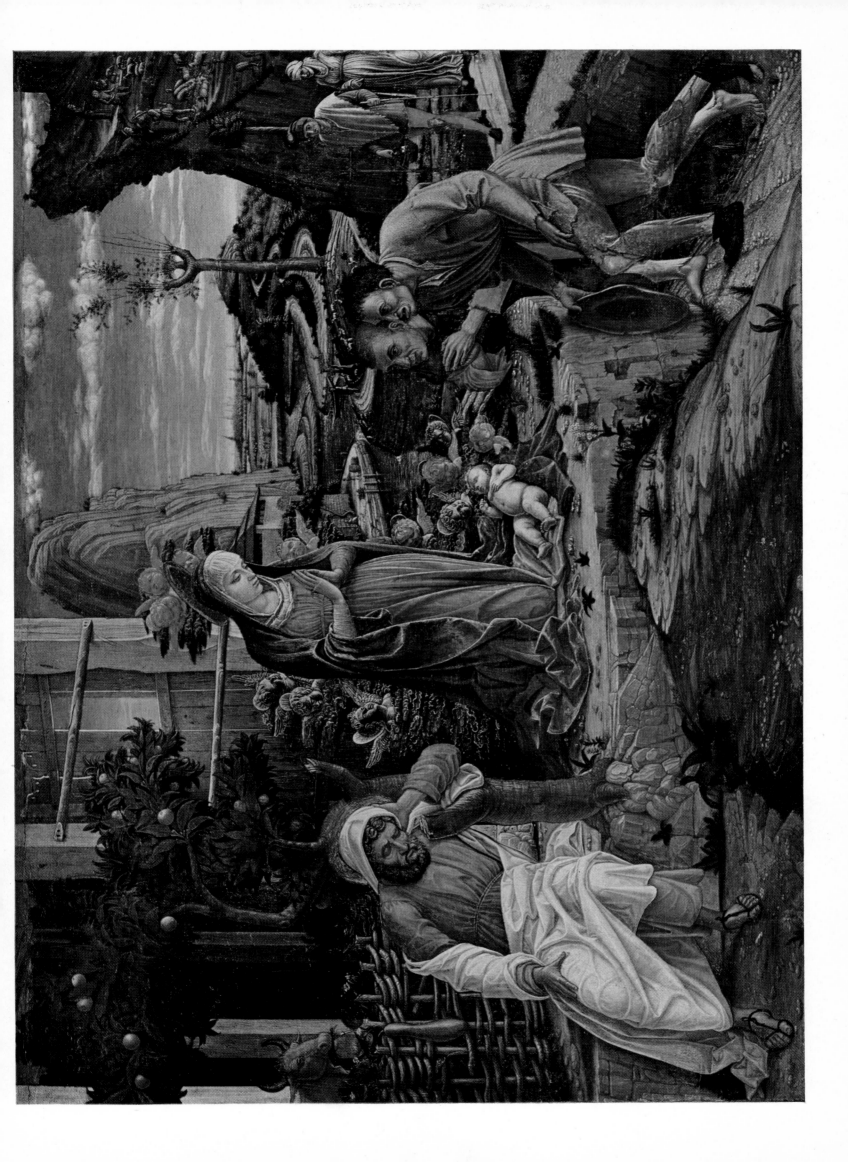

20 · CARLO CRIVELLI

Venice, active 1457-1493

MADONNA AND CHILD

Wood.   Height 14 in.; width 9 in.

BACHE COLLECTION. METROPOLITAN MUSEUM OF ART, NEW YORK

Carlo Crivelli participates in the trend of carrying to extreme the realization of material things, such as a piece of fruit, a brocade or a stone—a trend which stems from late Gothic taste. Mantegna, likewise, had the same tendency, but he framed and regulated it by the classical ideal of the Humanists. Carlo Crivelli disregarded any humanistic culture.

Educated in the Paduan milieu, very close to the young Mantegna, he abandoned Padua and Venice and lived for the greater part of his life in the southern part of the Marches, a region where no cultural center existed, at least none to be compared with Venice. There, furthermore, the only commissions for pictures came from the churches, and the clergy was steeped in tradition and dependence on Rome. It may well be that these conditions of life induced Crivelli to disregard humanistic ideals, if, indeed, he ever had them. In his painting one sees an ability to realize form and color which is similar to that of Mantegna, yet combined with a general conception of painting which goes back to the XIV century.

Crivelli was thoroughly familiar with perspective, but he very seldom used it. Often he even resumed a gold background. Proportions are again hierarchical, according to the importance of the image, not to its position in space. Anatomy is used not for the structure of a body, but for the accentuation of physical expression or for decorative values. Drawing is no longer a road to knowledge of reality, but it attains technical power and suggests the magic of art.

Because of its naturalness and grace, and its perfect state of preservation, and despite its small size, this Madonna is outstanding among Crivelli's works. The rhythm of his creation can be well followed in it. The parapet is of colored marble. It is decorated with sculptured motifs and is broken at one point. A carpet, bearing the signature of the painter, is laid on it. A fly is shown nearby; a cushion is placed over the carpet. All these elements are devised to furnish a seat for the child Jesus. The rhythm consists in the endless superimposition of elements. There is the same complication in the dress, in the halos, in the large pieces of fruit. Virtuosity is the main reason for it, yet is not the only one. The ideal of sumptuousness is overwhelming.

Crivelli had at his disposal much gold and perfect tints. His form makes that sumptuousness specific and emphatic. Thus his work serves the rich material and gives it a new power. To impress on the divine images an exceptional magnificence was for him a kind of religious rite. The seriousness of his undertaking is the proof of his sincerity. The intellectual value of his imagination can be disputed, but not the fascinating result of his conscientious work.

OPVS·KAROLI·CRIVELLI·VENETI

21 · ANTONELLO DA MESSINA

Messina, born about 1430, died 1479

PORTRAIT OF A YOUNG MAN
Wood. Height 12½ in.; width 10½ in.

JOHNSON COLLECTION. PHILADELPHIA MUSEUM OF ART, PHILADELPHIA

In the second half of the XV century, painters from all parts of Italy wished to realize humanistic ideals. Antonello came from Sicily. He had worked in and around his native town, but when he made a trip to Venice and Milan in 1475 and 1476 he was immediately considered a great master. The best Venetian painters followed him, including Giovanni Bellini, who was perhaps a greater artist than he.

A legend about him has spread from the word of Vasari in the XVI century: Antonello introduced into Italy the oil technique which he had learned during a trip to Flanders. Today we know that oil was used in Italian painting much before Antonello, and that he had been educated in Naples by Colantonio who was thoroughly acquainted with the technique and the style of the school of Van Eyck. One aspect of Antonello's art is indeed related to the Flemish way of painting. It is the realistic concentration on details and the ability to render the materials of things through gradation of colors. Mantegna, who dominated the taste of Venetian painting in 1475, did not know this gradation of color. Hence the success of Antonello among the painters was probably due to such modulation. At the same time the Duke of Milan appreciated Antonello's merit as a portraitist, through the vitality of his figures. Antonello also brought to Venice something else, a humanistic conception of form as tending to geometrical order, of composition as the perspective distribution of images in space. This order was even more evident and more sure than that in Mantegna, because it did not involve the contrast between humanistic form and Gothic coloring. It had the ability to unite form and color in a general rhythm of light and dark. Thus Antonello foretold the further development of Renaissance painting. This can be well seen in his Madonnas and in his famous St. Sebastian, but his main work consisted in portraits.

The portrait here reproduced shows Antonello's art at its best. The vitality of the face is more intense than that we see in life. There is something in its style which is abstracted from life in order to emphasize life. If we look at the eyes it is evident that the form of the eyelids is geometrical, more so than in reality. The same thing is true of the mouth and of the neck, which is like a section of a column. Moreover, the whole head is inscribed in an ideal cylinder. It is this geometrical accent which reveals the shrewd glance, the touch of humor in the mouth, the whole expression of intelligence and determination.

The planes suggest the ideal cylinder but depart from it to determine all the features in a continuous undulated rhythm without sharp contrast. This is due to the nuance of colors, which permits a precision of detail lacking in the more intellectual Florentine plasticity.

One must realize the historical importance of this achievement. It was a personal fusion of trends as different as those of Florence and Bruges, of the Renaissance and the Gothic styles, of Humanism and the Middle Ages. That this had to happen was destiny, but the fact is that it was attained in Venice in 1475 by Antonello.

22 · GIOVANNI BELLINI

Venice, first record 1459, died 1516

ST. FRANCIS IN ECSTASY

Wood. Height 48⅜ in.; width 55 in.

FRICK COLLECTION, NEW YORK

Marc Antonio Michiel saw this picture in 1525 in the house of Taddeo Contarini in Venice, and recorded that it had been painted by Giovanni Bellini for Zuan Michiel. Thus it appears that the picture was not created for a church but for a private amateur, who undoubtedly appreciated it not only for its religious but also for its pictorial value. This background of the work illuminates the real motive of the painter. Marc Antonio Michiel adds that the painting has "a landscape in the foreground admirably finished and studied." We thus learn that contemporaries valued not only the high finish but also the coherence, which is the fruit of the artist's research into the intimate nature of things.

The date of the painting must be around 1480, by which time Bellini had assimilated modulation of chiaroscuro from Antonello da Messina, abandoning the more linear style influenced by Andrea Mantegna in his early period.

This modulation unites all the elements of the picture, in spite of their minute finish. The devotion of the painter to the things represented does not injure his vision of the ensemble, because he is guided by a love of everything in nature, conscious that everything in this world is the creation of God.

The representation of St. Francis in Ecstasy suggests the moment when the Saint received the stigmata. Ever since the thirteenth century the scene of St. Francis receiving these signs of the Crucifixion had been repeated many times, as, for example, by Giotto. All these painters stressed the narration of the miracle and represented the winged cherub and the rays which produced the wounds. Giovanni Bellini, by contrast, translated the sacred legend into moral values. He represented the faith of St. Francis, his religious torment, his courage, his readiness for martyrdom. Thus his figure assumes a heroic value. He is alone in the wilderness with his conscience, and looks to heaven for inspiration.

About him everything is beautiful and gentle. Even the rocks assume delicate and precious colors. Nature is not the enemy of man but the friend. It is idyllic. The ass, the peacock, the shepherd, the castle, which people and enliven the landscape, are too beautiful to be wild and dangerous. Even the blue sky has some white clouds to diffuse serenity. Moral energy in man and lovely beauty in nature: these are the main elements of Giovanni Bellini's poetry. He is one of the greatest of Christian poets; one of the most sensitive painters of the Italian Renaissance.

He drew elements of his style from his father Jacopo, from his brother-in-law, Andrea Mantegna, from Antonello da Messina, and after 1500 even from the young Giorgione. But he remained always himself. He impressed on all the elements taken from other artists his sensibility, his humility, his moral energy and courage, and he transformed all those elements in a unity of his own.

Bellini painted his St. Francis in Ecstasy when he was about fifty, creating, in the full power of his maturity, one of his incomparable masterpieces.

23 · GIOVANNI BELLINI

Venice, first recorded 1459, died 1516

THE FEAST OF THE GODS

Canvas. Height 67 in.; width 74 in.

WIDENER COLLECTION. NATIONAL GALLERY OF ART, WASHINGTON

This painting, which is signed by the master and dated 1514, is a very famous one. It was executed for the Duke Alfonso d'Este of Ferrara to decorate a room in his palace, along with three bacchanals by Titian, now preserved in the Prado, Madrid, and in the National Gallery, London. Giorgio Vasari in 1568 said that "it is one of the most beautiful pictures that Gian Bellini ever painted." Nicholas Poussin was so impressed by it that he made a copy after it, now in the National Gallery of Scotland. Vasari added that Titian finished the painting. From the payment to Bellini in 1515 it would nevertheless appear that he had completed it. In the wood on the rock to the left there is, however, a freedom of brushwork which one does not expect from Bellini. The fact is that, as x-rays reveal, Bellini had shown at the left a forest of trees like that on the right; this part was then repainted in radically changed form by Titian.

The subject matter is derived from a passage in the *Fasti* of Ovid. "Cybele, with her brow crowned with turrets, invites to her feast the eternal Gods. She invites, too, the Satyrs and the Nymphs, Deities of the country. Silenus comes, though no one has invited him. . . . A sleepless night is spent over copious draughts of wine. . . . Vesta is lying down, and, free from fear, she enjoys quiet repose, her head, reclining just as it fell, on a tuft of grass." The illustration of the passage of Ovid is faithful in some details, as in the pose of Vesta at the right.

To understand the artistic character of the picture, however, one must keep in mind not only that Giovanni Bellini was a Christian poet, but also, as he pointed out to an ambassador of Isabella d'Este, that he could not follow too closely any fixed theme. He wanted to let his fancy wander freely.

The theme is a bacchanal with freedom of gesture and of desire, from an abundance of wine. However, the spirit of the scene is not pagan. There is no joy. The gluttony does not satisfy anyone. The figures are presented, rather than represented, as intent on a sacred rite, with the timidity which is proper to people who do not abandon themselves to an orgy. Their delicacy depends on an artistic style which was accustomed to paint Madonnas and Saints rather than drunkards. The sacred rite is enveloped in the mysterious dusk of the coloring, the woodland solitude, the distant echo of a yellow sunset. This suggests that the painter wishes to transform the bacchanal into a mysterious rite in which all nature participates. From the Christian consciousness of sin a romantic dream is born, which nullifies the classic theme and opens the way to a modern feeling for nature.

When Giovanni Bellini painted this picture he seems to have been more than eighty years old. His style had changed very much from that of his St. Francis in Ecstasy (No. 22) of 1480. The younger generation, headed by Giorgione, had shown the old master the way to a freer and more sensuous fancy. Giovanni Bellini assimilated a great deal of their new conception of coloring, of nuance, of light and shade. He also felt the necessity of going beyond human images in order to discover a feeling for nature. He did not renounce, however, his most essential character, his Christian seriousness and sweetness.

24 · JAN VAN EYCK

Maaseyck (Eyck on the Maas), born 1380-1390, died 1441

St. Francis Receiving the Stigmata

Wood.   Height 5 in.; width 5¾ in.

JOHNSON COLLECTION. PHILADELPHIA MUSEUM OF ART, PHILADELPHIA

This composition was twice painted by the artist: this is one version; the other is in the Turin Gallery. Although such an exact repetition by the same master may seem strange, a document of 1470 confirms that both are original works of Jan van Eyck. In that year Anselm Adornes, a man of Italian origin who was Burgomaster of Bruges, made his will. He left to his two daughters two small panels painted by Jan van Eyck representing St. Francis, on condition that two wings should be added to each panel with the portraits of himself and his wife. The Turin picture was found in a convent at Casale in Piedmont, the Johnson picture in Lisbon. A plant depicted in both paintings cannot be found in Flanders but only in the South of Europe, likewise the brown tunic was at that time worn by the Franciscan monks in Southern Europe, but not in Flanders, where they wore grey tunics. Jan van Eyck went to Lisbon in 1423 and remained there more than a year. One may surmise that he painted the two panels in Lisbon. It is possible, however, that he painted them afterwards recalling what he had seen in Lisbon. In any case the two paintings were in Bruges in 1470.

As is well known, Jan van Eyck greatly contributed to the artistic revival in Flanders, and is considered the founder of the Flemish school of painting. The traditional interpretation of the new style he promoted stressed his realism, his natural science, and the technique of oil. Today, however, his artistic character is viewed differently. He was no doubt a realist. But there are many kinds of realism, and one must try to define what van Eyck created in order to make his images appear real. He did not care for the structural aspects of reality, as one can see in the figure of St. Francis, whose feet are not in the same plan as the head and the hands. Nor did he care for the plastic quality of the figures, as one sees in the sleeping monk who forms an area of dark tonality which does not reveal the body under the tunic.

Van Eyck saw nature as an effect of light, colors and nuances. He was so full of enthusiasm for the individual color of a fabric, of grass, of a rock, of water and sky, that he defined the varying absorption of light by each material with a finesse unknown in his time. His depiction of the character of the surface of objects was and is unsurpassed. Of course this ability depends on a moral attitude of devotion to his work as well as to the appearance of things. It is this attitude which constitutes his greatness.

He did not imagine a general effect of light and shade, with all the details subordinated to it, but he invented a kind of subdued luminosity which could cling to the most different details and still permit all of them to participate in the unity of style. It is this subdued luminosity which reveals the supernatural vision of the artist, his mystical contemplation of nature, and which gives all his images a magical appearance.

Instead of concentrating his attention on man, the center of universe, as did his Italian contemporaries, he expounded his love of the whole of nature, and his serene optimism. It would seem that St. Bernard spoke for him when he said: "The whole earth is full of the majesty of God."

25 · JAN VAN EYCK

Maaseyck (Eyck on the Maas), born 1380-1390, died 1441

THE ANNUNCIATION

Wood (now canvas). Height 36¾ in.; width 14½.

MELLON COLLECTION. NATIONAL GALLERY OF ART, WASHINGTON

This is the right wing of a lost triptych. We learn that it came from Dijon, that it belonged to the collection of William II, King of the Netherlands, and subsequently to the Hermitage Gallery at Leningrad. It is one of the painter's masterpieces.

Van Eyck was a miniaturist and also a jeweller. The pictorial life given to inanimate things such as the cushion, the lilies or the prayer book, gives the painting a character of still life. The idea of representing the Annunciation in the interior of a church, instead of in a room or under a porch was one which had been anticipated by the miniatures of the Book of Hours of the Maréchal de Boucicault. The glitter of the pearls, the gold, the precious stones in the crown, in the mantle and in the sceptre of Gabriel, the splendor of color in the brocade of his robe and in the peacock feathers of his wings as well as in the dress of the Madonna, have never been surpassed.

These brilliant images find themselves in a subdued environment in a twilight which by contrast accentuates the sacredness of the event. The perspective is not rigorously scientific, like that of the Italian painters. It is intuitive, and by the nuances of the half shadows gives reality to the illusion of space. The style of the church is Romanesque. It recalls the cathedral and other churches of Tournai, but the painter did not imitate any single church. With devotion he created a building of his own. Following the idea of St. Boniface, the painter felt that a church is an image of Paradise. In the figured tile floor are represented stories foretelling the Redemption such as Delilah beheading Samson, Samson throwing down the pillars of the temple, David beheading Goliath. In the upper wall some indistinct scenes are suggested and in the window-glass a saint, perhaps St. Dominic. The light enters from numerous windows, always subdued, and does not envelop the figures, which are seen by their own light. The height of the church and its twilight suggest meditation and concentration.

The meaning of the figures is embodied, above all, in the brilliancy of their colors. Neither action nor a true relationship of feeling exists between them. Even the preciousness of the flesh tints suggests that the figures are sacred images of precious metal presented on an altar, rather than human beings. The smile of Gabriel is very pleasant but is stiff. It has been compared with that in the archaic Greek sculpture of Aegina. The Madonna expresses a devotion which is too naïve to be hypocritical. Her feeling is merely schematic, a type of feeling rather than an individual feeling.

All this, which has nothing to do with realism, suggests the artistic quality of van Eyck. His sensibility to every nuance of light, to the preciousness of colors, to the individual quality of any material, allows van Eyck to project his devotion into the smallest corners of his picture, that is, to impress any image with his astonished contemplation of the world, without distinguishing what pertains to heaven or what to earth.

26 · ROGER VAN DER WEYDEN

Tournai, born 1399-1400, died 1464

CHRIST ON THE CROSS WITH THE VIRGIN AND ST. JOHN

Wood. Two panels, each: Height 70 in.; width 36¼ in.

JOHNSON COLLECTION. PHILADELPHIA MUSEUM OF ART, PHILADELPHIA

These two panels probably decorated the external face of the two shutters of a triptych. Their proportions explain the division of the two episodes: the Christ on the cross on one panel, the Virgin and St. John on the other, instead of the usual arrangement with figures at the two sides of the cross.

From this practical necessity, however, Roger van der Weyden developed an artistic purpose, that of isolating the figures in order to intensify their plastic qualities as well as their expression. The darker drapery behind the light figures emphasizes by contrast their relief and their isolation. It concentrates the attention on them. This results from the artist's desire for simplification and concentration. The lines are elaborate and vibrating, both in the draperies and in the bodies. This is true especially in the nude figure of Christ, but the simplification remains. The vibration of the lines emphasizes the torment and the anguish of the figures.

The trend of Roger van der Weyden is exactly the opposite to that of van Eyck. Van Eyck cares for everything on earth. He finds his expression through a rich sensibility for nuances, which enlivens all detailed elements. He sees and loves above all what is attractive and alluring. Roger, on the contrary, concentrates his powerful sensibility on the sacred images, discarding everything else, which exists only in order to enhance the power of the images. Finally, he agitates and distorts the images in order to glorify their dramatic expression. The calm and serenity of van Eyck is transformed by Roger into a deep concern for religious sorrow and repentance. The marvelous balance between the divine and the earthly is broken. Only the divinity—the spiritual, the moral struggle—appear to the eyes of Roger van der Weyden.

It has been said that such an artistic conception is a backward step by comparison with van Eyck's art, a step from the worldly to the churchly, from the beginning of the Renaissance back toward the Middle Ages. This opinion however does not take into account that the Renaissance was not a movement against religion, but one with a new trend in religious feeling. Roger van der Weyden's feeling no longer belongs to the Middle Ages. He is too conscious of the sorrow and torments of mankind. He completely projects the divine into the moral conscience. He forecasts that state of mind which paved the way to the Reformation.

Ever since the time of Van Mander in the XVII century, Roger has been appreciated for his representation of the soul, its sorrows and its passions: his artistic expression is indeed dedicated to tragedy. Observe the skull at the foot of the cross, how desperate it is; all the torments of hell are concentrated in those eye pits. This skull can be considered a key to the intimate nature of the form of Roger, the tragic accent of his whole expression. It is a commentary both on the form of the loin cloth of Christ and on the swooning of the Mother of God.

27 · ROGER VAN DER WEYDEN

Tournai, born 1390-1400, died 1464

PORTRAIT OF A LADY

Wood.   Height 14½ in.; width 10¾ in.

MELLON COLLECTION.   NATIONAL GALLERY OF ART, WASHINGTON

This portrait comes from the ducal house of Anhalt-Dessau, at Worlitz. The sitter has not been identified but it has been supposed that the portrait represents Marie de Valengin, illegitimate daughter of Philip the Good of Burgundy. Its date has been surmised to be around 1455.

Very few portraits by Roger van der Weyden remain, but we know that he painted many of them, and became a fashionable portraitist of his time. In spite of this, what impresses us in Roger's portraits is his severity. He is not interested in presenting the charm of a young and probably virtuous woman. If we regard a portrait by Jan van Eyck we observe that even in the image of an old man he suggests his joy of life, his sympathy for everything living. Roger van der Weyden could not express in a portrait his tragic conception of life, but he was too conscientious to express feelings in which he could not share. Hence in his portraits he discarded any feeling, and concentrated his attention on the visual likeness. His way of reaching this likeness, however, was characteristic of him: a simplification of all details, an exceptional firmness of plastic form, a strong contrast of light and dark zones, the isolation of the central motif. Thus he created the image of a woman sure of her self, straightforward, reserved, with a strong will, and with severe morals. She can be the daughter of a king, and become a queen; she can be also a nun, but, if so, she will certainly become an abbess.

Of course all this is only the projection of the state of mind of Roger van der Weyden into the image of his sitter. All his portraits show such a strong will, the only characteristic which remained when the tragedy of religious life was discarded. Certainly it was this expression of determination, together with the obvious likeness, which explains the success of Roger's portraits.

28 · DIRK BOUTS

Haarlem, first recorded 1445, died 1475

MOSES BEFORE THE BURNING BUSH

Wood. Height 17⅛ in.; width 13⅝ in.

Dirk Bouts follows the passage of Exodus (III, 2-5) closely: "God called unto him (Moses) out of the midst of the bush and said, Moses, Moses. And he said, Here am I, And He said, Draw not nigh hither; put off thy shoes from off thy feet, for the place whereon thou standest is holy ground."

The artist represented two different moments of the event, as was common in the narrative painting of the Middle Ages. In the middle distance Moses is taking off his shoes. Behind him are the sheep he has been guarding. In the foreground Moses has approached the burning bush and is kneeling to God who announces to him that he must guide the people of Israel out of Egypt towards the Promised Land. With raised hands he shows his agitation at such an announcement.

This painting must have been quite a famous one, because both Albert Bouts and Quintin Massys imitated it.

In the XVI Century Molanus wrote that Dirk Bouts was renowned as the inventor of landscape painting. No pure landscape paintings by Dirk Bouts are known, nor are the landscapes he painted for his religious scenes more developed than those of Jan van Eyck or Roger van der Weyden. In criticism today it is not invention but creation which matters. Dirk Bouts was creative in feeling the value of space and the relationship between figures and landscape in a personal way and with a greater intensity than had any of his predecessors. His landscapes are outstanding because of the finesse of color nuances and the effects of light which give a new unity of vision. This step towards the subordination of the single colors to the general effect of light is important not only in itself but also because it forecasts the contribution to painting made by Dutch artists, particularly in the XVII century.

In order to emphasize the third dimension of his landscapes, Dirk Bouts scattered figures on different planes. Here the repetition of the images of Moses accentuates the depth of vision. The painter conceived depth of space in a similar composition, his Harvest of Manna, part of the Sacrament altarpiece in St. Peter's, Louvain.

In spite of his Dutch origin Dirk Bouts belongs to the Flemish school. He is a follower of Roger van der Weyden, from whom he drew his desire for simplification and expressiveness. But his temperament is very different from that of Roger and he does not feel the urge to drama. His love of nature and his sympathy for human beings made him closer to van Eyck. However he does not express the joy of life, nor ecstasy at the splendor of the universe. His muse is sadly pensive and leads to an elegiac metre. This is the mood which unites figures and landscape, and which impresses his landscape with a serene melancholy.

29 · HANS MEMLING

Region of Mainz on the Rhine, born 1430-35, died 1494

THE WIFE OF TOMASO PORTINARI

Wood.   Height 17⅞/₁₆ in.; width 13½ in.

ALTMAN COLLECTION.   METROPOLITAN MUSEUM OF ART, NEW YORK

Tomaso Portinari was an Italian merchant, a resident of Bruges. He commissioned Memling to paint his own portrait and that of his wife, which ultimately went from an Italian collection to the Metropolitan. In addition, Portinari wanted a painting with all the scenes of the Passion. Memling painted this on a panel, also with the portraits of Portinari and his wife, now in the Turin Gallery.

Memling had great success as a portrait painter in Bruges, above all among the Italian merchants in that town. He had felt the influence of Roger van der Weyden, and reached Bruges when he was a mature painter. During his life his success was great. After his death, however, his renown declined and remained at a low level until the Romantics began searching for primitives. They rediscovered Memling and extolled him as the greatest Flemish primitive after van Eyck.

Today we explain his success in his lifetime by other qualities. He was engaging, respectful of social conventions, ready to satisfy the sense of class distinction and the pride of his clients. He also had very refined technical skill. As for the Romantics, they often confused sweetness of expression and devotion to workmanship with a really religious feeling. Memling was their man. In his portraits he never carried to an extreme an insistence on individual character of the sitter, or lost the sense of reality in order to emphasize idealized grace. He followed a middle way, and became outstanding among his contemporaries in the realization of order, of rhythmical composition, of subtle drawing, of pure and smooth color. In other words, he was master of all the secondary qualities of a painter but his creative power was limited. His originality consists not in a new conception of life and style, but in the refinement of what had been created before him, above all by Roger van der Weyden.

A comparison with the Portrait of Lady by Roger (No. 27) shows that the image of the wife of Tomaso Portinari is more delicate. It is also weaker. Perhaps, being of German origin, Memling learned the Flemish style as he would a foreign language, and used it with an academic touch, as an external ideal, not born in his own veins. In spite of his shortcomings, he created many masterpieces.

30 · GERARD DAVID

Oudewater (South Holland), born before 1460, died 1523

THE REST ON THE FLIGHT TO EGYPT

Wood. Height 17⅜ in.; width 17⅜ in.

MELLON COLLECTION. NATIONAL GALLERY OF ART, WASHINGTON

This was painted after 1509, the date of another picture by the same artist in the Museum of Rouen, with the same figure of the Christ child. The image of St. Joseph, gathering chestnuts, is derived from a miniature in a Flemish manuscript. This painting must have been renowned: it was imitated by Ysenbrandt, among others, in a picture in the Philip Lehman collection, New York. It belongs to the mature style of the master.

The coloring is intense and precious, but it is subordinated to a general effect of light and dark zones. The unity of tone so long sought by the Flemish masters after van Eyck is here thoroughly realized. The end of independent details is thus in view. At the same time the sense of monumentality is well expressed by the isolation of the group of the Madonna and Child. It is detached as a dark zone against the light tone of the ground. There is thus a pictorial rather than a plastic effect which could have demanded a light tone against a dark one. The group is inscribed in a square which contributes to its monumental appearance. The work is a presentation of images, rather than the representation of an event. Instead of depicting the episode of the rest on the flight into Egypt, David presents images of the Madonna and Child, with the grapes that are a eucharistic symbol. Only in the background does one see the ass, and St. Joseph gathering the chestnuts. The elements of the event must be gathered together by the imagination of the observer. This is typical of symbolic reference as opposed to narrative representation.

The ideal of the artist is a kind of beauty, intentionally naïve, full of youthful grace, too fresh and clear, too extended to the whole earth and the sky, to be melancholy. The rest on the flight is Gerard David's own rest, a natural escape from any intensity of feeling. It is a repose full of satisfaction in work well done.

Gerard David was a pupil of Memling, and learned from him his calm, well measured grace. One sees in David, however, a creative power, a moral certainty greater than in his master. On the other hand Gerard David copied from many masters, van Eyck, Roger, van der Goes. The reason for his copying so much was probably not a lack of invention, but a preference for continuing tradition, a respect for tradition, and, above all, a concentration on the execution of his painting. He did not dare try any adventure in art.

Even when he introduced something of the Italian Renaissance style in seeking monumentality and balance, he did so in the most prudent way. It would seem as if Gerard David achieved everything he wished because he sought only what he could accomplish perfectly well. With him a great period of Flemish painting comes to an end.

31 · HIERONYMUS BOSCH

Herzogenbosch (Holland), born about 1450, died 1516

THE ADORATION OF THE MAGI

Wood. Height 30½ in.; width 22 in.

This painting, which comes from the collection of the Earl of Ellenborough, is considered to be one of the earliest works of Hieronymus Bosch, and shows the first impulse to depart from the tradition of the Netherland school of painting, of van Eyck onward.

This Adoration of the Magi can be compared with that in the Munich Gallery by Dirk Bouts, the master who, more than any other predecessor, has some affinity with Bosch. Bouts, however, takes the sacred legend very seriously, and explains step by step the story of the event, the offer of the gifts, and the adoration of the Child. Bosch, on the contrary, seems to take nothing seriously, and sees in the sacred legend only a pretext for a comic fancy. The older King who is kneeling and offering a gift seems to offer only a toy. The Madonna and the Child are so thin that they appear mere phantoms. The second and the third Kings are waiting for their turn, while they have a little chat together. St. Joseph has just become aware of their presence and hurries towards them with an awkward gesture, since a good tavern keeper must not leave his guests alone. But if Bosch cannot take human figures seriously, whether saints or devils, he has the greatest respect for nature. In the landscape the delicacy of colors and lights is extreme. It expresses a finesse of lyricism: the straw thatch and the distant town are marvelously done, with a sympathy which is allied with the artist's great skill.

Bosch was born in a provincial town, where he did not find a great school of painting, thus he was not bound to an important tradition. The feeling around him was popular and vulgar, hence his pleasure in the comic. The church could not impose its tradition of reserve and dignity. The motif of Bosch is constantly comic and popular. But his form has nothing to do with popular art. He is not only refined and certain but is also a precursor of modern art. The glorious principles of the school of van Eyck had, with Memling and David, reached the end of their vitality. Something new was necessary to embody the coming trends of emotion and thought. Bosch had a deep religious feeling for nature, but not for the puppets the Church offered for adoration. Hence he mocked them, and left his fancy unbridled. No devilry could satisfy his hunger for the grotesque.

His success was great. Princes bought his works. Cardinal Grimani of Venice owned some of them. Later, around 1550, a revival of the taste for them took place: numerous painters imitated him and Philip II of Spain was fond of him. Many of those who praised Bosch believed, as did Guicciardini, that his works were mere fantastic whimsies. But Giorgione thought it worth while to assimilate the delicate gradations of his colors in landscape. Fray Joseph de Siguença, in a book published in 1605, defended Bosch from charge of heresy and suggested that by his satire on sins and human inconsistency he was able to paint the intimate soul of men, while other painters represented only the external appearance.

Fray Siguença had modern ideas of criticism; he was sufficiently unprejudiced to find spiritual values under comic forms and motifs. In modern times everyone of course agrees with him, and the surrealists extol Bosch as their greatest forerunner. Indeed he was able to find a deeper spiritual truth in a nuance of color or in a fantastic line than other painters who obeyed the rules of the Church.

32 · RAPHAEL

Urbino, born 1483, died 1520

THE SMALL COWPER MADONNA

Wood.   Height 23 in.; width 17 in.

This Madonna was bought by Lord Cowper in Urbino about 1780 and remained in the Cowper family at Panshanger, Hertfordshire, until 1913, when it was brought to the United States.

It was painted about 1505, approximately at the time of the Granduca Madonna in the Pitti Gallery in Florence. The church shown in the background recalls that of San Bernardino on the outskirts of Urbino.

When Raphael painted it, he had assimilated the chiaroscuro and the *sfumato* (shadowy mistiness) of Leonardo da Vinci. His composition was based on *contrapposto*, a sort of balance among the parts of the bodies, permitting them to appear in movement within the contour of the group, which is peacefully tranquil. Raphael's interest in plastic quality was very keen. Thus he painted the brown landscape behind the dress of the Madonna and the sky behind the flesh tints, maintaining an effect of light on dark tones. Raphael was enabled by the example of Leonardo to attain the intellectual refinement of Florentine art. He came, however, from the school of Perugino, that is, from an interpretation of Florentine forms based on Umbrian sentimentality. Hence his ability to enliven the intellectuality of the Florentine with exquisite feeling. We must emphasize that the ideal of Raphael was beauty, and that his genius beautified everything he touched with exceptional ease. The fusion of these elements, the artistic knowledge of the Florentines, the sentimental sweetness of the Umbrian, and Raphael's own creative power of beauty, explains the incomparable grace of this Madonna.

The Granduca Madonna is more intellectually idealized than this one. Other Madonnas by Raphael are more monumental. None is so lovely. Perhaps this is because, while he was already thoroughly master of his form, he still remembered his Urbino, where he was born. The church of San Bernardino in the background is a proof of it. And he still remembered his Perugia, where he was born to art, and the sweet modesty of Perugino's Madonnas. Thus in the small Cowper Madonna the perfect form envelops a naïve feeling of grace. Hence an ecstatic contemplation of beauty which is not transcendental but deeply rooted in the earth. This is a mother and a child, whose divinity consists in their beauty and in some suggestions of a simple, debonair moral feeling. Rarely has the sense of divinity been so embodied in physical appearance. All those who have not been touched by a mystical impulse have found through the centuries and still find in this Madonna the perfect fulfilment of their need of an ideal.

33 · RAPHAEL

Urbino, born 1483, died 1520

ST. GEORGE AND THE DRAGON

Wood.   Height 11¼ in.; width 8⅛ in.

Guidobaldo da Montefeltro, Duke of Urbino, commissioned this painting as a gift to Henry VII of England. Count Baldassarre Castiglione, author of *The Courtier,* brought it to the King. Guidobaldo had been honored with the Order of the Garter and Raphael depicted on the St. George the insignia of the order. On the horse's harness he signed his name: RAPHELLO. V., that is, Raphael of Urbino. A drawing for this picture is preserved in the Uffizi at Florence.

This panel passed from the English royal collection to the Earl of Pembroke. Later it belonged to the collection of Charles I. It was then taken to France, and bought from the Crozat collection by Catherine the Great for the Hermitage Gallery at St. Petersburg, now Leningrad.

The picture was painted by Raphael in 1504-1505, with special care, for the ruler of his native town. It is perfectly preserved. Almost contemporary with the small Cowper Madonna, it shows a different aim. Instead of beauty and grace in a young woman and in a child, one here sees beauty and grace in movement and action.

The white horse which occupies the center of the picture is arrested, as the subject matter requires, but still maintains its previous spring. The plastic roundness of the back of the horse, and its frightened eyes, however, while they do not contradict the movement, are seen for their own sake.

Certain dark zones, such as the dragon and the armor and the mantle of St. George, contrast with the white horse, but have not the function of shadows. They are juxtaposed and constitute organic unities, with their own light and dark colors. This suggests that Raphael liked a coordinated composition, where every image was a complete work of art, with its own different beauty.

St. George is not only the warrior who kills the dragon, but also a very pleasing young man who does not reveal any effort in the struggle. His face is calm and sweet. He is the blond prince, a young girl's ideal. The dragon wants to be a horrid and frightening monster, but is not. In this connection one must recall the ideas of St. Augustine on the divine beauty of a monkey, when its parts are well adapted to characterize a monkey. The princess saved by St. George is an attractive praying saint, the hill around the grotto is very gently colored, the foliage of the trees is illuminated by touches of gold, the sky is pure, clear and serene.

Those who demand from a picture such as this the representation of a fight, the expression of energy and hatred, will be disappointed. What Raphael wants to paint is a representation of the marvelous, where everything reveals its preciousness. It would appear that creative imagination can produce in painting a kind of preciousness which is much beyond that of jewels. This is the case in this little picture. Nothing can exceed it.

34 · GIORGIONE

Castelfranco Veneto, born about 1480, died 1510

THE ADORATION OF THE SHEPHERDS

Wood. Height 35¾ in.; width 43½ in.

In 1540 Taddeo Albano, the ambassador of the Gonzaga to the Republic of Venice, wrote to Isabella d'Este Gonzaga concerning two paintings by Giorgione in Venetian collections. Both represented "una Nocte," that is, a Nativity or an Adoration of the Shepherds. This picture is perhaps one of them. From the collection of Cardinal Fesch in Rome, which was sold in 1841, the picture passed to that of Claudius Tarral. In 1847 it was purchased by T. Wentworth Beaumont and, later, by Lord Allendale of London.

This is the best preserved of the religious paintings by Giorgione. It was probably painted between 1500 and 1505, when Giorgione was still impressed by the Christian feeling of Giovanni Bellini. Later he preferred to dedicate himself to fantastic art, such as his Thunder Storm, the Three Philosophers or the Venus, without any precise subject matter. In this picture one can observe the very moment when Giorgione transformed traditional subject matter into a dream—a sacred legend into pantheistic contemplation of nature.

The moment chosen is when night is vanishing and day is not yet born. Before a grotto in a rock, apart from the life of nature, figures appear like phantoms. The plastic qualities, dear to the XV century artists and above all to the Florentines, are disregarded. Giorgione sees differently. Touches of color here and there are submerged in a general half-shadow. Interrupted and enveloped, the figures, touched by vivid colors, appear and disappear. They are suggested rather than described and acquire an appearance of unreality. Their feelings of piety are revealed by the dream-like atmosphere which lets the souls appear more than the bodies. Lights and half-shadows are very warm, and emphasize the sensuous quality of this expression of adoration. The suspension of any action, the moment of silence and meditation, retired from the tumult of nature: this is the poetry of Giorgione. In the distance nature is on the point of being awakened by the light of dawn.

As a painter-poet Giorgione creates a world to be contemplated with humble devotion and sensuous love. As a pure painter he profits by all the experience of previous art. Proportions and sense of reality come to him from the Florentines; the love of half-shadows is inspired by Leonardo; the nuances of color, as well as the interaction between figures and landscape, are suggested by Giovanni Bellini. Certain distinctions in the relations between materials and their reaction to light are due to Flemish tradition known in Venice probably from paintings by Bosch. Giorgione, however, knew how to fuse all these different elements by giving them a new unity of light and shade and a new meaning. He subordinated all his forms and colors to his fantastic dream. It is the dreamlike nature of his images that makes of him one of the greatest artists known to history, and one of the greatest forerunners of modern painting.

35 · TITIAN

Pieve di Cadore, born 1477, died 1576

PORTRAIT OF PIETRO ARETINO

Canvas.   Height 39½ in.; width 33¼ in.

FRICK COLLECTION, NEW YORK

Until the beginning of this century this painting hung in the Palace of Prince Chigi in Rome.

Pietro Aretino, the writer, was a friend and a promoter of Titian, who made at least two portraits of him. In addition to this one there is another, preserved in the Pitti Gallery, Florence. That was painted in 1545 so that Aretino could send it to Cosimo, Duke of Florence. In a woodcut on the title page of the *Lettere* by Aretino published in Venice, 1538, a drawing by Titian is reproduced showing a bust of Aretino very similar to the head of the Frick picture.

In a letter of October 17, 1545, Aretino says that the Pitti portrait is very much alive, but is too sketchy, above all in the reproduction of the clothes. The Frick picture is more sketchy than the one at the Pitti, and probably satisfied Aretino even less. But one must remember that Aretino profited from the paintings by Titian to get money, and his judgment depends on the salability of the picture. Then as now a painting reproducing a fabric exactly and objectively is more appreciated in the market than a sketch, but this factor has no relation to art.

The artistic quality can be understood by a comparison of the Frick painting with the one at the Pitti. In the latter Titian portrays Pietro Aretino in a movement which reveals the strong personality of the sitter at the very moment of his life when he was painted. Baudelaire said that a portrait can be poetry or history. No doubt the Pitti portrait conforms to the nature of history. Historians of art have indeed been tempted to read into this historical portrait the intelligence, the sensuality, the vice of Pietro Aretino, and have appreciated the painting for its wonderful power of psychological representation. Its artistic quality, which is of course very great, has been somewhat passed over.

The Frick picture has less psychological character. The face is strongly built, but has no particular significance. The whole body is not in movement; it is presented as a rich volume of colors rather than represented as an individualized moment of life. Titian cares less for his sitter and more for his painting. Thus he does not paint the history of a famous and vicious writer, nor a document of XVI century Venetian life; he paints a great pictorial effect, where transparencies and reflections, touches of light and nuances of half-shadow create a whole of outstanding magnitude. It emerges from the surrounding atmosphere with a subdued contour line, with a continuous transition, so that even the solid body participates in the mystery of aerial beings. It is not the image, it is the painting that breathes. The pictorial effect is complete and perfect, but beyond it Titian's imagination develops a lyrical contemplation. That is, the pictorial and the poetical effect coincide. This portrait conforms to the nature of poetry.

Aretino insinuated that Titian had not reproduced the fabrics in his portrait exactly enough because he was not paid enough. We now realize that the sketchy character of the Frick painting was necessary to the immersion of the image in the surrounding atmosphere, because any precise contour or any detailed modeling would have destroyed that. By his sketchy treatment Titian thoroughly expressed his own pictorial ideal, and anticipated, as well, the pictorial taste which in the XIX century ended in Impressionism.

The ideal of Titian was connected with his admiration for the aristocratic way of life. He had become acquainted with this through the influence of the Spaniards, who in his day had made themselves masters of Italy. When he visited Charles V and his court he was impressed by the solemnity, the richness, the aristocratic expression of the great Spaniards. His style bears the mark of his admiration, and impresses it on the sumptuosity of that mass of colors which portrays Pietro Aretino.

36 · TITIAN

Pieve di Cadore, born 1477, died 1576

THE RAPE OF EUROPA

Canvas. Height 70 in.; width 80½ in.

This painting, signed TITIANUS P., was made for King Philip II of Spain. From the letters of Titian we know that it was begun in 1559, finished and sent from Venice to Madrid in 1562. It belongs to a group of "poems" (Titian called them *poesie*) including Venus and Adonis, Diana and Callisto, Diana and Actaeon, The Death of Actaeon, Perseus and Andromeda, most of them preserved in various collections in London. The first of them, however, is still in Madrid, in the Prado. Philip V of Spain gave our painting to the Duc de Grammont, from whom it passed into the collections of the Duc d'Orléans and of the Earl of Berwick. It was purchased by Mrs. Gardner in 1896.

During the XVII and XVIII centuries it was greatly admired by painters such as Rubens, Van Dyck, Rembrandt, Watteau and Reynolds. All these painters were indebted to Titian, who in his later period brought the pictorial style to an extreme of brilliancy and coherence which has not been surpassed. The Rape of Europa is perhaps the most daring of his compositions and one of his freest examples of execution. Hence its great fame and success.

The composition is wholly in depth. The foreshortening of Europa, her diagonal position, the placing of the group of Europa and the bull in one corner, create a cubic space where the images appear. The eye of the observer is attracted towards the sky, the rocks and the sea. There is a sort of haze, in tune with the portentous mythological event by its menacing mystery. The cupids have the visual function of balancing the composition in depth by suggesting the presence of the surface. Their psychological function is to relieve the mythological marvel by a playful touch. However it is the presence of nature, with its distant horizon and its nebulous appearance, which expresses the state of mind of the painter.

Europa is in full movement, as though she were borne away by the wind rather than the bull. Her forms are still plastic enough to show the effort of the movement, the impulse of a will for action. But in the landscape, as well as in the flying veil, the movement is not connected with action. It is a cosmic vibration closely interwoven with the nuances of light and shade. This is the artistic movement that enlivens the whole painting and suggests the supernatural.

The cubic space is therefore filled by a cosmic vibration rather than by figures. This modifies the whole conception of painting, by comparison with what had been done before. Not only is man no longer the center of the universe, as he was in XV century Florentine painting, but he is only one element of nature. This is the discovery of nature in painting; it is the pendant in art of what later became pantheism in thought. This discovery is connected with the subordinations of all images to light. The colors in The Rape of Europa are extremely subtle and delicate, not by their single qualities, but because they form a harmony of light and shade. Hence a new subordination of all elements to the chosen one—light—and a new unity of form and motif.

The subject matter has lost all interest for the painter. The king of gods, Zeus, transformed into a bull, bears Europa from Phoenicia to Crete—Europa who will become the mother of Minos. A distant rock or the flying veil have a much greater importance in the painting than the subject matter. Titian has no faith in the gods, nor in man; but he remains ecstatic before nature. This attitude is the root of his creative power and of his discoveries in the world of art.

37 · CORREGGIO

(Antonio Allegri called Correggio)
Correggio, born before 1489, died 1534

The Mystic Marriage of St. Catherine

Wood.   Height 52⅖ in.; width 48⅗ in.

DETROIT INSTITUTE OF ARTS, DETROIT

The first mention of this painting was when it was in the Gonzaga Gallery in Mantua. It was subsequently in the collections of King Charles I of England, of Pope Pius VII, and of Prince Kaunitz, Chancellor of Austria. After the sale of the latter's collection and after passing through various Viennese ownerships, it came to the Detroit Institute of Arts in 1926.

The painting well represents the earliest style of Correggio, around 1514, and shows how deeply he was influenced by Leonardo da Vinci. The *sfumato*, that is, the mistiness of the shadows, was a treatment inaugurated by Leonardo, to surpass the purely plastic quality of the Florentine XV century tradition. Everyone understood that his contours were smoother and more delicate than before, and that they gave to the faces he painted a new grace, an exquisite sensitiveness, a poetical mystery, which accounts for his great success. On the other hand Leonardo's impulse to make an ideal of the *sfumato* was his principal of the "universality" of painting, that is, the necessity of representing not only man but the whole of nature, even the rain and the stars in the sky, which could not be represented by a plastic image. It was an intellectual aim, a desire for knowledge, which guided Leonardo towards the *sfumato*.

Giorgione had realized a similar ideal through colors (see No. 33). Correggio adopted the manner of Leonardo, but with a different temperament. He was not a really intellectual man and profited by the *sfumato* only to achieve graceful images, foregoing any problem of knowledge.

Correggio lived in a small town, where life was provincial, and the urge for familiar affection was very strong. Thus he transformed the Mystic Marriage of St. Catherine into a familiar scene. It could be called a genre scene, if a genre painter had ever reached the artistic level of Correggio. St. John the Baptist, St. Anne, St. Joseph smile at the prowess of a child; the Madonna is moved by contemplating the child Jesus, who amuses himself with the finger of St. Catherine. The latter shows a moral consciousness of the great event. The delicacy of gradations on her face creates a delicious grace. From a pictorial point of view St. Anne is the best image; shadows and half-shadows play over her face with Rembrandtesque fantasy. All images, and the landscape as well, participate in this general vibration of light and shade which has lost the character of representing reality, and has acquired the value of a happy fancy. It is a subdued joy, a moment of satisfaction for the familiar gathering, a parenthesis in a life of melancholy.

Under the *sfumato* the colors are veiled but still vivid. They echo the preciousness of the Paduan and Ferrarese tradition. The forms are absorbed in the effect of light and shade but show themselves to the extent necessary to reveal the smiling grace.

Correggio was, if not the most admired, certainly the Italian painter most beloved by the European artists of the XVII and XVIII centuries. His fame, however, was due to the works of his later period, where his grace is more developed and sure. Today we prefer his earlier works where we note less certainty, but more intense creativity, a greater concentration of soul even in a smile.

88

38 · TINTORETTO

Venice, born 1518, died 1594

PORTRAIT OF NICOLÒ PRIULI

Canvas.   Height 44½ in.; width 35 in.

FRICK COLLECTION, NEW YORK

This painting comes from the collection of the Dukes of Abercorn, Belvoir Park, Down, Ireland. The identification of the sitter as Nicolò Priuli rests on comparison with a portrait of him in the Ducal Palace, Venice, bearing the initials and the arms of Priuli. That is less powerful than the Frick portrait, either because it was executed by a pupil of Tintoretto, or because it belongs to a later time, as a memorial picture of a man dead many years before. In fact Nicolò Priuli was Procurator of Saint Mark in 1545 and died in 1549. The Frick picture shows, therefore, the style of Tintoretto at his great moment, when he painted the Miracle of Saint Mark (1548) in the Venice Academy.

In 1545 Jacopo Robusti, called Il Tintoretto, who had been a pupil of Titian and had left his studio some years before, was distinguished by Pietro Aretino, the writer, as a master of "brevity," that is, of conciseness. The rapidity and freedom of touch which created this brevity appeared to the eyes of the Renaissance as negligence and carelessness. Today, however, we understand that without that freedom of touch, that so-called negligence, the whole pictorial effect of Tintoretto would be lost. If you compare the fabrics painted by Jan van Eyck (No. 24) with those of the portrait by Tintoretto, you will be convinced that the style is different and that the effect obtained by Tintoretto does not exist in van Eyck— and vice versa. There is neither progress nor regression; there is only a change of taste.

Hence it is necessary for a critic to avoid the ridiculous demand for a little more diligence in Tintoretto, and to try to understand the aim, the intimate coherence, of that negligence.

Art and artisanship were confused during the Middle Ages. In the Italian Renaissance the pride of the artist distanced the artisan. Careful polish and detailed precision in painting were the mark of the artisan. Dolce in 1557 advised the Venetian painters to avoid too much diligence. This is the meaning of Tintoretto's "brevity."

The painting of the Venetian senator is one of the most finished among Tintoretto's portraits. Clothes and background, however, are subordinated to the most important element, the face framed by the white beard. The evocation of the face is thus emphasized, by comparison with that of other elements. The Aretino portrait by Titian (No. 35) has no such contrast. The appearance of Tintoretto's image is much more vigorous than that of Titian. Moreover the color scheme of Tintoretto is almost elementary in comparison with that of Titian. To the nuances of tone of the latter, Tintoretto opposes contrasts of tone; to the large volume of a body enveloped by the atmosphere, he opposes an image sharply detached from the background. Contrasts and detachments in painting mean a dramatic effect. Of course Tintoretto's portrait does not represent any dramatic action, but the very appearance of the image is dramatic. Behind the loggia, the lagoon, the island of San Michele, the boats with their sails swelled by wind, suggest the life of the past, when the old senator was young. This is an added touch to the pathetic figure of the old, but still powerful, seaman.

Tintoretto's image is also more direct. It has not the lyrical mediation of the image of Titian. This too is the mark of a dramatic effect, which fully justifies the brevity, the contrasts and the detachments in their coherence with the whole.

39 · VERONESE

Verona, born 1525, died 1588

MARS AND VENUS

Canvas.   Height 81 in.; width 63⅜ in.

This painting, signed "PAVLVS VERONENSIS. F.," was mentioned by Ridolfi (1646) as made by Veronese for the Emperor Rudolf II, and was described in an inventory of Rudolf's collection as Mars, Venus and cupids with a horse. Later it belonged to Queen Christina of Sweden, to the Dukes of Orleans, to various collectors in Rome and London. It was finally purchased in 1910 for the Metropolitan Museum of Art. The date of the picture can be fixed between 1576 and 1584, when Borghini mentioned it in *Il Riposo*.

The subject matter has received various interpretations, such as the Adoption of Hercules by Juno, or Chastity transformed by Love into Charity. But the inventory of Rudolf's collection speaks of Mars and Venus, and Veronese painted other scenes with the same theme (for example one in the former Gualino collection). Moreover Veronese's indifference for complicated and concealed symbolism is well known. Mars and Venus was a good pretext for his composition of colors.

Paolo Caliari, called Il Veronese, was educated in his native town, Verona, and came to Venice when he was a mature painter. In spite of the strong influence of Titian's pictures, he never lost his independence from the main current of Venetian painters. Titian and Tintoretto had subordinated their interest in single colors in order to attain a total unity. Veronese put his accent on the brightness of single colors. Titian and above all Tintoretto did not abstain from dark colors in order to emphasize contrasts of light. Veronese cared for light only in so far as it could harmonize his colors, hence his palette is lighter than that of the others. He was not interested in dramatic effects, nor in sacred Christian legends, but only in the attractiveness of forms and colors. He became the greatest portraitist of Venetian life of the second half of the XVI century. It was a good life, calm, rich and hedonistic, although it was losing its former energy. The only creative impulse which remained came from the pleasure of contemplating nature. The painter had command of all resources: the forms were varied and distinguished, the composition in depth was easily realized, poses were chosen not as representing an action, nor as accentuating the aspect, but as elements of a pattern. No movement either of bodies or of souls, but continuous changing of poses for variety and vivacity. It is an art for art sake, saved by a lively creativity and limited by a conventional luxury. What is important is the fantasy of color. One must observe the colors to enjoy the luminous body of Venus and the half shadows around Mars. Abstracted from color the composition would become artificial and rhetorical.

Instead of a faith in God or life, Veronese offers his ideal of good manners. Empty of any moral content, they transform any sacred or profane event into a social one, capable of appealing to the fashionable life of his time. The pleasure of contemplation is the only motif of the picture.

40 · EL GRECO

Fódele (Crete), born 1541, died 1614

The Assumption of the Virgin

Canvas.   Height 158 in.; width 90 in.

ART INSTITUTE OF CHICAGO, CHICAGO

The work is signed in Greek: "Domenikos Theotokopoulus painted this picture A. D. 1577." It was made for the high altar of Santo Domingo el Antiguo, Toledo, Spain. Subsequently it passed to the Museo Nacional de Fomento, Madrid, to Don Sebastian Gabriel de Bourbon and to Infanta Doña Cristina of Spain. In 1904 it was acquired for the Art Institute of Chicago.

It is probable that this Assumption was the first picture El Greco painted in Spain. In the years immediately following he integrated it with the Trinity in the Prado Museum, Madrid, the Resurrection and the Adoration of the Shepherds, both still in their original places in Santo Domingo el Antiguo, Toledo.

This was the ensemble which established the fame of El Greco in Spain, the Assumption being the most important piece of the whole. It was perhaps the first time he had such a large canvas to cover. Although foretelling his individual style, he epitomized in it what he had assimilated in Italy. The grand style, the centering of the figure, the free movement of the images, an organized disorder, a relationship between the single colors and the general effect of light—for all this his models were Titian and Tintoretto. The elongated proportions, the ideal forms, the sharp contours were inspired by the Roman mannerists. But El Greco, before going to Venice and Rome, had been acquainted with late Byzantine painting, which taught him to rely on imagination for art without caring for control by nature, and to enjoy single colors for their own brilliancy. The Byzantine and the Italian traditions had no longer anything in common in the second half of the XVI century. Only a daring genius such as El Greco could profit from both and through their synthesis find a personal style.

Under his brush the single colors were again emphasized, but with understanding of their function in the effect of light; forms were freed from the experience of reality, after having fully realized that experience. Thus a new consciousness arose of the distinction between art and nature, art acquiring a greater independence than it had had during the Renaissance. The whole baroque style can be understood as a declaration of the rights of imagination, and El Greco greatly contributed to it. This reveals the primitive side of the art of El Greco. Even Tintoretto, who was the spirit most akin to him, was too tied to Italian civilization to dare to break with it. Moreover, on arriving in Spain, El Greco felt the mystical ambience which eased the escape from nature, even if in that mysticism there was a great deal of display. He did not choose with subtlety among the components of his picture, he accepted all, and mingled them. His genius was too great to let him fail. It transformed the possible lapses of taste into pictorial discoveries. Any form which was too distinct became an accent of life, any dissonance of colors suggested a new harmony, any emphatic gesture was a pretext for fancy.

Pacheco, one of his contemporary admirers, spoke of El Greco's "cruel blurrings." Paravicino said that he was an "emulator of a more intense life" and suggested that Jupiter, the lord of heaven and the god of light, to punish him, hurled a lightning-bolt upon his colors making them look like "burning snow." Beyond these baroque images El Greco's creativity freely flies.

41 · EL GRECO

Fódele (Crete), born 1541, died 1614

Portrait of Cardinal Don Fernando Niño de Guevara

Canvas. Height 67¼ in ; width 42½ in.

The artist signed the picture in Greek: "Domenikos Theotokopoulos made it." Niño de Guevara (1541-1609) was made a cardinal in 1596 and in 1601 left Toledo for Seville. El Greco painted him between these two dates. Originally this portrait hung opposite Guevara's tomb in the Convento San Pablo Ermitaño in Toledo. It then belonged to certain Madrid collections until it was bought by Mrs. H. O. Havemeyer, New York, who bequeathed it to the Metropolitan in 1929.

The Assumption and Niño de Guevara were offered to Mrs. Havemeyer in 1905. The second was preferred in spite of its greater cost. Perhaps in the time of El Greco the Assumption would have been preferred. Mrs. Havemeyer, however, had formed her taste on the Impressionist masters, and as a forerunner of Impressionism the Niño de Guevara was far superior. In the Assumption there was still a subject matter which, to exalt the Catholic religion, required some conventional features. In the portrait, on the contrary, nothing came between the eyes of the painter and the subject matter. Even the dignity of a cardinal did not matter. The painter enjoyed the special red of his robe and harmonized the flesh tints, the tunic, and the background with that red. The harmony is based on contrasts. The red is luminous, varied, brilliant, self-imposing, challenging. All the rest is dull, neutral, self-concealing in order to exalt the red.

If one compares this portrait with those of Tintoretto (No. 38) or Titian (No. 35), one becomes aware of the intellectual values proper to the Venetian images, of their structure, of their just position in space. Nobody can demand the same values of El Greco. His impulse in exalting his red is such that he disregards any intellectual rule in vision. He thus loses a great deal, but he acquires much, too. The vividness of his image is incomparably superior to that of the Venetians. This is a good example of the quality an artist can reach by refusing to follow an intellectual tradition, by forgetting what he has learned, in order to exalt his sensation.

If the eyes of El Greco are concentrated on the red, his mind is concerned with the character of the sitter. Being a Greek he was impressed by the different appearance of the Spaniards. It was the time of the height of the Spanish Inquisition, with its prudence and its cruelty. A high dignitary of the church in Spain was for him a great inquisitor; behind his spectacles he appears as an ideal type of the investigator.

The same creative rhythm was responsible for the challenging red and for the profound expression. It was a rhythm full of energy, of concentration, of simplification, going straight to its goal.

No image can appear more real than this. But one must not forget, that this reality is so emphasized because El Greco's imagination went beyond reality and attained types, the red and the cardinal, which are abstract from reality. The study of reality, of its different aspects, of its relations, would have brought a retarding of the effect. Paravicino spoke of El Greco's "intense life;" today we can speak of his "impulsive life."

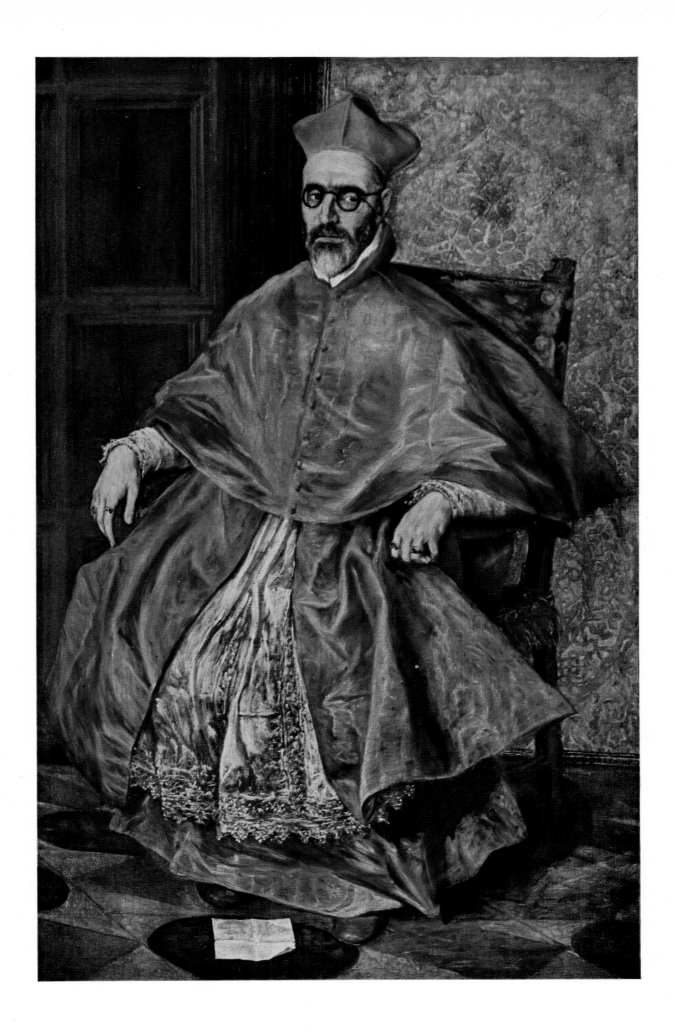

42 · EL GRECO

Fódele (Crete), born 1541, died 1614

VIEW OF TOLEDO

Canvas. Height 47¾ in.; width 42¾ in.

Again there is a signature in Greek: "Domenikos Theotokopoulos made it." The inventory of the goods of the son of El Greco, Jorge Manuel, made in 1621, mentions two views of Toledo by his father. Both are known. This is one: the other is preserved in the Museo del Greco, Toledo, Spain. During the XVIII century the Metropolitan picture was probably in Madrid in the Capocavana chapel of the Convento de Religiosos Agustinos Recoletos. Then, through a Madrid collection, it reached that of Mrs. H. O. Havemeyer, who bequeathed it to the Metropolitan in 1929.

The view of Toledo which is preserved in the Museo del Greco aims at objective representation. A plan of the town was added to the view by the painter. The Havemeyer view, on the contrary, has no topographical aim but only an artistic one. The view is taken from across the Tagus, but as has been noted, the actual arrangement of the city's buildings was sacrified. Thus Toledo is only a pretext for a fantastic creation.

Landscape paintings had received from Giorgione a new content, that of expressing the mood of the artist, aside from the human figures which people them. Following Giorgione, Titian and Tintoretto had contributed to this humanization of nature, and emphasized the effect of light as unifying all the things represented in a fantastic whole. But El Greco has something new to say.

Above all, he disregards perspective. His lines aim at a pattern on the surface, and only the color tones suggest distance in depth. This does not mean that the artist creates a real space: near and far belong to a visionary suggestion rather than to a representation. The touches of light and shade in the foreground forecast the impressionistic style, that is, they disregard the structure of things and are content with the simple appearance. The contrasts of light and dark zones increase in the middle distance, and the accents of light on the buildings transform reality into a dreamlike vision. Farther on, the dark mountain is under the spell of a cloudy sky, where the menace of a storm becomes grandiose and epic.

The impressionistic style used in the foreground is abandoned in the background for a dramatic effect. In a few inches of painting El Greco makes the step from impressionism to expressionism. Not only does he enliven nature, but he expresses through lights and clouds the fear of man of a cosmic explosion. If in the portrait of Niño de Guevara his simplifications and his accents emphasize a real life, in the View of Toledo he reaches a pure world of fancy where the only nature is the feeling of man. This is one of the best examples of the visionary moments of El Greco, when he penetrates the mysteries of the universe, and experiences in his own soul all the tortures that romanticism brought to mankind two centuries later.

45 · VELASQUEZ

Seville, born 1599, died 1660

PHILIP IV AT FRAGA

Canvas. Height 51¾₁₆ in.; width 39¾₁₆ in.

FRICK COLLECTION, NEW YORK

When Philip IV of Spain went to Aragon in 1644 in order to put down the revolution of Catalonia, Velasquez followed him and painted this portrait at Fraga. Philip V sent the portrait to the Dukes of Parma. It was brought to Wartegg Castle, Switzerland, in 1859, and then to Schwartzau Castle and Liechtenegg Castle, Austria. It became part of the Frick Collection in 1911.

Among the numerous portraits of Philip IV painted by Velasquez there are two which show the king in his dignity as commander of the army, although he had not yet taken part in any war. One of them, begun in 1628 and hanging in the Prado, Madrid, shows him on horseback. The other in which he is arrayed in armor, with sash and baton, was sent to England in 1638, and hangs at Hampton Court. By 1644 Philip IV for the first time found it necessary to engage in war. At Fraga he wanted to be portrayed not only as a commander but in the full splendor of royalty. For this reason none of the other portraits of the king has such a colorful and luxurious aspect as the one in the Frick Collection. Only certain portraits of his Queen Anna Maria and of the Infanta Maria Teresa can be compared with this one for brilliancy of coloring.

In 1644 Diego Rodriguez de Silva y Velasquez had reached his full maturity and mastery of his means. His first trip to Italy, in 1629-1631, had broadened his experience in the matter of coloring and had suggested a lightness and ease which he had lacked in his early period. His self-restraint, however, called for a precise frame for the fireworks of the precious colors. Thus the dark background and the black hat determine the planes between which the colors can have their freedom. These two dark zones, by contrast, allow the brilliant colors to explode. But even in the brilliancy Velasquez maintained his reserve: the tone which unites the various colors is silvery not golden. Hence the fantastic aristocracy of the impression.

For Velasquez, as well as for Holbein, critical tradition stresses the objectivity of his art. Carl Justi, the most famous of his biographers, says, for example, that Velasquez among all portraitists is the one who paints himself the least. If this were true, the style of Velasquez would be the least recognizable, while the contrary is the case. Justi himself adds that his style is that of pride, and this is perfectly right. To say his style is one of pride means that Velasquez detached himself from the model in order to reveal his own reserve, his intellectual superiority, either to a king or a buffoon.

The illusion of the objectivity of Velasquez depends on his extraordinary power of impressing life on everything he painted, whether a face or an embroidery. This power is indeed one of the most outstanding in the whole history of art.

46 · PETER PAUL RUBENS

Siegen (near Cologne), born 1577, died 1640

THE HEAD OF CYRUS BROUGHT TO QUEEN TOMYRIS

Canvas.   Height 80 in.; width 141 in.

MUSEUM OF FINE ARTS, BOSTON

This painting once belonged to Queen Christina of Sweden; then, in the XVIII century to the Dukes of Orleans, then to the Earl of Darnley of Cobham Hall. In 1941 it was purchased by the Museum of Fine Arts, Boston.

The picture is believed to have been painted around 1623. The grounds for this assumption are that the two boys at the left are Rubens' two sons, Albert, born in 1614 and Nicholas, born in 1618. As represented, they appear to be about nine and five years old. The dog in the arms of the figure at the left was represented by Rubens in the decorations of the Luxembourg palace for Maria de' Medici, now in the Louvre, which were executed between 1621 and 1625.

The subject matter is taken from Herodotus. He relates how Cyrus tried by treachery to conquer the territory of the Massegetae, the kingdom of Queen Tomyris, but was finally defeated and slain. The head of Cyrus, covered with blood, was brought to Tomyris. Two other paintings by Rubens of the same subject, differently treated, are mentioned by Rooses: one in the Louvre, the other a grisaille in the Léon de Barbure Collection, Antwerp.

Peter Paul Rubens was not only a great painter but a great man. History does not record another painter who had such enormous success, social as well as diplomatic. No other painter produced so many large canvases. He had the help, it is true, of a great number of pupils, but he had the ability to impress his own creative power on all his canvases. He gave a powerful impetus to the development of the baroque style in painting; indeed, he impersonated the pictorial baroque in Europe. Although he assimilated a great deal from Italian painting, he distinguished himself from other painters under Italian influence by his preference for the Venetian rather than the Roman style, thus happily anticipating the further development of painting in Europe. Thereby, he transcended the contrast between the Flemish and the Italian traditions, achieving in his own style a synthesis of both.

Many critics, however, have objected to his heroic achievements because of the sensuousness, the heaviness and the pompousness of his compositions. He had no classic taste, no rigor, no reticence, no moderation. His art is based on impulse, energy, abundance, improvisation. His too ample women, above all, offend a refined taste. Such critics do not understand that roundness, abundance and ostentation are elements necessary to Rubens' impulse to creation. One cannot have one without the other, yet his creative power cannot be denied by any rule of taste. His contemporaries understood him better and praised his work as a whole.

The Head of Cyrus Brought to Queen Tomyris is a perfect example of his state painting. Rubens did not care for the drama inherent in the story told by Herodotus. What interested him was the marvelous coloring, the variety of human forms, masterfully moulded and full of life, the crowd of vigorous people who enjoy the triumph of Tomyris and disregard the head of Cyrus. Though the subject matter is the head of Cyrus offered to Tomyris, the motif of Rubens is a great pageant. It must be judged as a pageant. As such, it is perfectly convincing. Many beautiful women and many strong men gather together in a crowd which is moving with the same rhythm as the columns, with the sole aim of dazzling the beholder. Virtuosity seems to dominate, but as all effort is lacking, one feels the ease and the joy of creation, which is true art. It is an art of expansiveness, not of concentration, but in its way it is a miracle of genius.

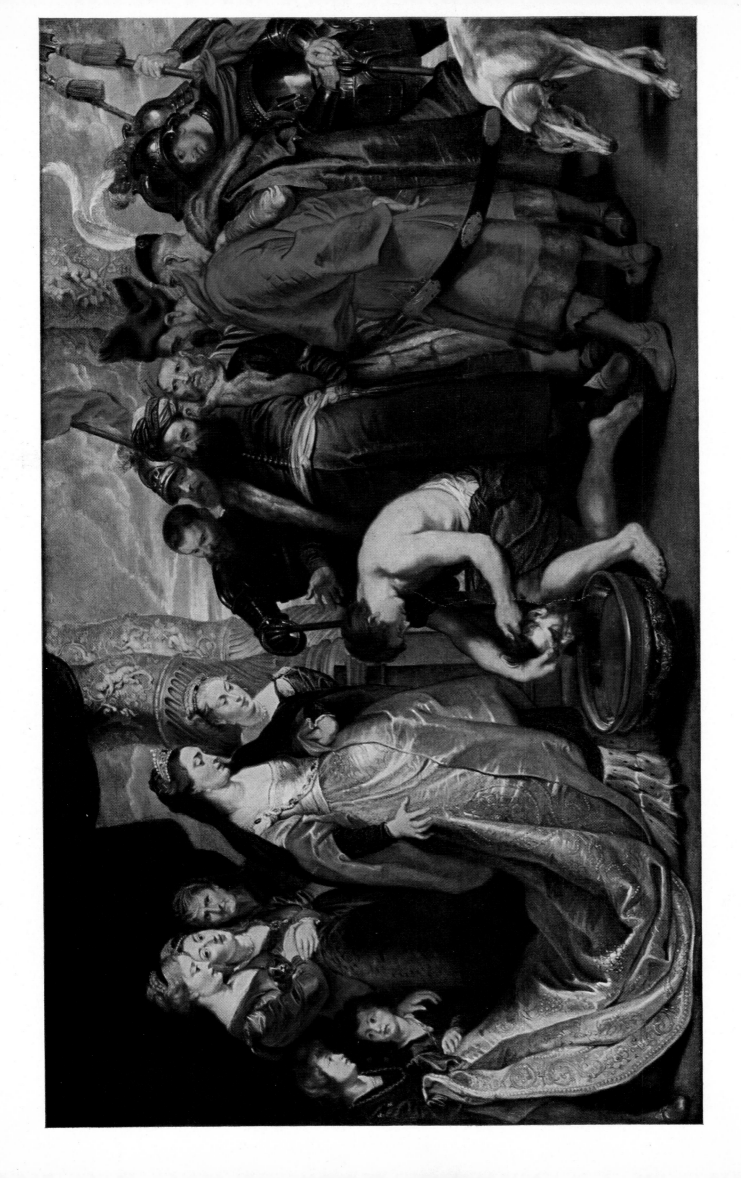

47 · PETER PAUL RUBENS

Siegen (near Cologne), born 1577, died 1640

THOMAS HOWARD, EARL OF ARUNDEL

Canvas. Height 54 in.; width 45 in.

ISABELLA STEWART GARDNER MUSEUM, BOSTON

An old English manuscript, a "Catalogue of the Works of Art in the possession of Sir Peter Paul Rubens at the time of his decease," mentions "the picture of the Earl of Arundell, upon cloth." This may be either the Gardner picture, or a portrait of the same subject in the National Gallery, London. In 1763 the Gardner portrait was engraved while in the possession of the first Greville, Earl of Warwick. The fifth Earl sold it, and Mrs. Gardner bought it in 1898.

Rubens portrayed the Earl of Arundel several times. He visited the Earl in London in 1629, and then painted the Gardner portrait, as well as the one in the National Gallery. There is also a drawing of him in a private collection in Brussels. In Antwerp, in 1620, Rubens had painted a large canvas with a group including the Earl, his wife, a dwarf, a dog and a buffoon. It was, before the war, in the Alte Pinakothek, Munich.

Thomas Howard, second Earl of Arundel (1585-1646) belonged to the family of the Dukes of Norfolk. Rubens represented him with the badge of a Knight of the Garter and with the golden baton of the Earl Marshal or Lord High Constable of England. After having served the royal family with varied fortunes he retired from public life and died in Padua. His fame rests on his collection of antiques, which was the first great collection in England.

Some of Rubens' greatest masterpieces are portraits. This may seem very strange in view of his decorative, baroque style, where he gave free rein to his rich imagination. But one must take into consideration the fact that Rubens always wanted to be a realistic painter. Even in his religious scenes, he introduced figures from his environment, drawn from life. On the other hand, his imagination often supplied some manneristic elements, particularly rounded forms and pompous movement. It is only natural that he was compelled by the likeness of the sitter to restrain his imagination, to concentrate on one figure only, instead of permitting his creative power to embrace a whole crowd of figures, architectural elements, landscape and so on.

It is doubtless difficult to find in a portrait by Rubens the expression of the individual character of the sitter. Rubens was too interested in life in general, too enthusiastic over the presence of his model, and he was content to render the energy of aspect.

The Earl of Arundel is shown in a dignified pose, with the attributes of command: the golden baton, the rich armor, and the helmet. The movement, the foreshortening of the body, the varying direction of body and face, the light which dwells on the armor and fades away in the background—all this is done to accentuate the vigor of the image. Rubens found all these pictorial elements in the portraits of Titian, which he studied with great care, but he carried this sort of portraiture to its extreme consequences, enhancing the vitality of the image, even if he lost the distinction and the reserve which constitute the characteristic of Titian.

Thomas, Earl
of
Arundel.

48 · ANTHONY VAN DYCK

Antwerp, born 1599, died 1641

MARCHESA ELENA GRIMALDI, WIFE OF MARCHESE NICOLA CATTANEO

Canvas. Height 97 in.; width 68 in.

WIDENER COLLECTION. NATIONAL GALLERY OF ART, WASHINGTON

The Cattaneo Palace in Genoa continued to house this painting until it came to the Widener Collection at the beginning of this century. In 1828 Andrew Wilson tried to buy the picture for the National Gallery, London, then in its beginnings, but the Cattaneo family was not willing to part with it at that time.

The date at which it was painted is probably 1623, at the very start of Van Dyck's second trip to Italy, perhaps the greatest moment of his creative power, when his fame was already established.

Elena Grimaldi Cattaneo was a beautiful young woman with the most aristocratic manners of the nobility of Genoa, at a period when Genoa was a great center of wealth and art.

Anthony Van Dyck owed largely to Rubens his baroque conception of art and the richness of his coloring. He was indebted to Titian for the subtlety of the coloring and gradations and for the distinction of his images. Van Dyck's nature was full of grace and aristocratic delicacy, which Rubens did not possess. It was only natural that Van Dyck should find in Titian many a suggestion to deviate from Rubens' path and to develop his own ideal of aristocratic grace.

Of course what exists in the feeling of a painter is reflected in forms and colors. The ideal of aristocracy contributed to a greater unity of tone and color by comparison with that of Rubens. The reserve in feeling became a reserve in coloring. The baroque style called for a subordination of all the components of a picture to the one chosen as the leading element. In other words, it called for a rigorous unity of general effect. By seeking greater unity, Van Dyck took a further step towards the attainment of the full baroque style.

The ideal of aristocracy was a social ideal, but the ideal of unity was visual. Both contributed to the great fame of Van Dyck, and made his works the models of fashionable portraiture throughout Europe for two centuries.

The portrait of Elena Grimaldi Cattaneo is one of Van Dyck's greatest achievements. She is shown walking out of a palace, accompanied by a negro servant who holds a red parasol over her. Van Dyck makes use of the parasol to reflect some red on the flesh tints. The Marchesa is dressed in a black costume. Van Dyck makes use of this also to enhance by contrast the light color of her face and hands. The background is a theatrical scene: high columns which rise beyond the limits of the picture, a staircase, a hilly landscape and a cloudy sky. All this furnishes a romantic setting for the appearance on the stage of a goddess of Genoese society.

It is difficult today, after all the troubles mankind has had since the end of the XVIII century, to appreciate fully the image of a life so proud of its external appearance. But if we enter into the atmosphere of that life, we are able to admire the grandeur both of Anthony Van Dyck and of Elena Grimaldi Cattaneo.

49 · FRANS HALS

Mechlin, born probably 1584, died 1666

PORTRAIT OF CLAEST DUYST VAN VOORHOUT

Canvas. Height 31¾ in.; width 26 in.

This portrait of Claest Duyst, the proprietor of the Zwaan Brewery at Haarlem, Holland, comes from the collections of the Earls of Egremont, of Colonel Egremont Wyndham, and of Lord Leconfield, Petworth, Sussex.

It was painted about 1636, in Hals' most brilliant period, before the influence of Rembrandt and old age led him to concentrate on expression and renounce his vivacious coloring. This portrait represents the most individual and characteristic qualities of Frans Hals.

The first reaction to Hals' style was perfectly expressed in 1714 by François Halma: "His work seems to speak by its shadows and half-shadows, it seems even to be moving. These indeed are qualities even more praiseworthy than the precise contour of the finishing." Frans Hals had been educated in a manneristic tradition; the passage from a manneristic plastic form to one based on light and shade was his own work. It was quite independent of Italian influence. It was a one man revolution.

This can be explained by the character of the artist. His youth was joyous, with a great deal of *laissez aller*, and an absence of moral constraint. His ability to realize in painting what he saw and wanted is almost unique in the whole history of art. Hence the ease and lightness of his touch. To offer a likeness, and to enlive it, was child's play for him. What he portrayed was neither the intimate soul of the sitter, nor the inner construction of his body. We do not know that Frans Hals ever painted a nude. He was content with the outward appearance of people, but within this limitation no one has surpassed him in making the image come to life. He was fond of how people looked, and one can feel his sympathy for his sitters. They are often smiling, because to smile is to live, and they are looking straight ahead, without any inner thought—with a boldness relieved by a touch of humor. Hals did not care for objective beauty, nor for the beauty of a line or a form. What he enjoyed was the harmony of colors and, above all, the nuance of a subdued light in any color. His form was never sculptural. He stressed the external appearance of the image without any roundness. By his emphasis on the aspect, on the effect of light and on the surface he was a chief forerunner of Manet and the Impressionists. It was at the beginning of Impressionism that the fame of Frans Hals was reestablished and rose higher and higher.

It has been observed that, in spite of his realism, Hals viewed his images in abstract schemes of lines: hence the primitive touch underlying his virtuosity. The absence of any moral or religious element in his paintings likewise suggests that his revolution in visualizing was accompanied by a detachment from the humanistic tradition and an adhesion to the rationalistic conception of life impersonated by Descartes.

His new vision of a life detached from the moral and religious tradition, and his consciousness that his was a new beginning, were the roots of Hals' poetry and art. They permitted him to transcend his tremendous virtuosity and to create an impress of terrifying vitality.

50 · REMBRANDT

Leyden, born 1606, died 1669

THE POLISH RIDER

Canvas. Height 45½ in.; width 52⅗ in.

This painting, which bears a fragmentary signature of an R on a rock, was probably bought in London in 1790-1791 for Stanislaus II Augustus (1732-1798), King of Poland. It was included in his collection which was sold to Prince Drucki-Lubecki, then to Count Jan F. Tarnowski, the founder of the gallery at Dzików. It remained there until 1910 when it became part of the Frick collection.

Connoisseurs of Rembrandt agree in fixing the date of the picture at the beginning of his last period, that is in the 'fifties.

It is one of the most, if not the most fantastic creation of Rembrandt, where visualization and mood perfectly coincide. The origin of such an image has been analyzed by Julius S. Held so thoroughly that one can but summarize his conclusions. The painting represents an Eastern soldier of the light cavalry. He may be Polish, Hungarian, or of another Eastern country. Rembrandt may have been inspired by an actual soldier whom he saw in Holland, or he may have dressed his figure with the oriental arms and clothes he liked. All that is certain is that he wished to represent an Eastern horseman.

The light Eastern cavalry had great renown in the XVII century. Their heroic deeds saved the Western countries from invasion by the Turks. The character of "Miles Christianus," of the fighter for the faith in the midst of darkest dangers, gives the spiritual origin of the rider of Rembrandt.

As for the formal conception, one must remember that Rembrandt was acquainted with the eleven circular etchings by Stefano della Bella representing Polish, Hungarian, Turkish and Moorish mounted soldiers. Not only the general theme is shared by the etchings and by Rembrandt's painting, but some of the details are, as well.

There is, moreover, a drawing by Rembrandt, representing a skeleton rider, preserved by the Darmstadt Museum. It was suggested by one in the anatomical theatre at Leyden, probably at the time Rembrandt was preparing his Anatomy of Dr. Johannes Deyman, of which only a fragment remains in the Amsterdam museum. His drawing of a skeleton rider has a connection with the Polish rider in the form of the horse as well as in certain characteristics not precisely definable. One thing is certain: the dramatic appearance of the Polish rider depends partly on the impression received by Rembrandt from the skeleton rider of the anatomical theatre.

Finally, the sculptured King on Horseback of Bamberg Cathedral, and the engraving by Durer representing Knight, Death and the Devil must be taken into consideration as antecedents of Rembrandt's creation.

Rembrandt, to be sure, transformed all these elements into a new artistic whole through his gradations of half shadow.

Out of a mist, veiling a mountain and a castle full of menacing dangers, appears a young soldier. He rides the horse of death. He is young and confident. He looks only toward his own ideal as if toward the sunrise. He follows his destiny, unaware that his destiny is to have the death of a hero. What the half shadows stamp on him, as well as on the surrounding atmosphere, is the fanciful nature of the painting. Such a soldier is a phantasm, the likeness of an ideal of heroism and adventure. The moment of poetry in painting is of unsurpassable spiritual height.

Leyden, born 1606, died 1669

PORTRAIT OF A LADY WITH AN OSTRICH FEATHER FAN

Canvas. Height 39 in.; width 32½ in.

Rembrandt signed this painting with an incomplete date which has been interpreted as being 1667. It came from the collection of Prince Youssoupoff, Leningrad. The companion piece, portraying the husband of the sitter, is also in the Widener Collection at the National Gallery of Art in Washington. It has many affinities of style with his Sindics, of the Rijksmuseum in Amsterdam, dated 1661-1662.

The portrait of a Lady with an Ostrich Feather Fan thus belongs to the latest style of Rembrandt. After having lived through many troubles, even disgrace, he created his finest masterpieces and surpassed himself. He has acquired a new simplicity. He no longer tries to model his pictorial style on the picturesque in life, and intensifies the precious quality of his colors. Nothing can be simpler than this portrait: some zones of light and dark colors against a half-shadowy wall, a straight, frontal half figure. This is all. There is no virtuosity.

The woman is about forty years old. She is well dressed and dignified, with a touch of melancholy, she has no physical beauty. The work, however, has a beauty, which is due to light and nuance, but which is something more. She is a living creature with her soul apparent on her face and in her pose. This visualization of what cannot be seen, a mysterious, magic power, is the art of Rembrandt at his best. The beauty of the woman, like that of the aged Rembrandt, is a moral beauty.

The difference between physical and moral beauty is the same as that between plastic and luministic style. A plastic quality is so materialized that it has been called a tactile value—a value of touch. It shows all the components of an image coordinated in a whole, but each component has its individuality. In the luministic style, on the contrary, all the components are subordinated to the light, which cannot be touched, and the whole of the image is much more rigorously united. A figure painted in a plastic style is always static even if it is in a pose of movement, while a figure painted in a luministic style is always moving even if the pose is static. Rembrandt's movement is a cosmic vibration of modulated half shadows, creating the movement of his figures, but independent of them, because it exists everywhere, even on heavy things such as a wall. This does not mean that the image of the Lady with an Ostrich Feather Fan has not its solidity, the dress around the neck or around the wrists emphasize the volume of the figure. But it is an atmospheric volume, a revelation of a phantom, which cannot be touched. It is vibrating with the perennial movement of an inner life. What must be revealed and what must be concealed does not depend on the objective model, but on the imagination of the painter. When the painter has Rembrandt's insight, he concentrates on revealing what other people do not see, the human soul.

53 · JAN VERMEER

Delft, born 1632, died 1675

YOUNG GIRL WITH A FLUTE

Wood. Height 7⅞ in.; width 7 in.

WIDENER COLLECTION. NATIONAL GALLERY OF ART, WASHINGTON

Abraham Bredius discovered this painting in 1906, in the house of Jonkheer de Grez, Brussels. It had been inherited from the family of van Boxtel en Liempe, of Bois-le-Duc, Holland. Through the August Janssen collection at Amsterdam it reached the Widener Collection.

Thus before 1906 a painting such as this, so precious as an object of art, so intense in the expression of life, was considered a nice little painting of an anonymous master. This was the destiny of almost all the paintings of Vermeer before Thoré-Bürger, in an article in the *Gazette des Beaux-Arts* in 1866, revealed to the world of amateurs the greatness of the painter. Thoré-Bürger asserted that Vermeer was the greatest Dutch painter beside Rembrandt, and today everyone believes this. Some even maintain that Vermeer is a purer painter than Rembrandt himself. There is no doubt but that Vermeer is the greatest colorist of the Dutch school, and one of the greatest colorists of all time.

The harmony of his colors is daring. His yellows and blues go together very well because his yellows are cold and whitish and his blues are subdued and atmospheric. The key of his harmony is a silvery light, as contrasted with the whole tradition of golden blondness from the Venetians to Rembrandt. Vermeer's half shadows assume the preciousness of a pearl. This is what everyone sees in a painting by him. It seems strange that his countrymen failed to see it and soon forgot their best colorist while they remembered so many other good practicians.

The fact is that the Dutch people of the XVIII century admired their painters because they revealed their everyday life as though in a mirror. They praised them insofar as their portrait of the country was a faithful one. The only exception was Rembrandt. This was because of his romantic dream, which opened for the Dutch people an unknown world. Vermeer, however, was too similar to the other painters of genre scenes for people to see that his painting was of another kind, or for them to be aware of his ideal values. As a portraitist of everyday life Vermeer was less faithful than Metzu or Pieter de Hooch. When we look at the best paintings of Metzu or Pieter de Hooch we become aware that their coloring is less cold but quite as precious as that of Vermeer. It does not impress us, however, as does that of Vermeer. It does not appear so miraculous.

Here it must be emphasized that the difference consists in the form. Whereas the form of Metzu or Pieter de Hooch is adroit but conventional, the form of Vermeer is the perfect structure of the harmony of his coloring. The Young Girl with a Flute is a marvelous example of it. Consider the foreshortening of the figure; it is sufficient to occupy space in depth. The figure is not in the center of the surface. Thus figure and atmospheric space constitute a well united whole. On the other hand, the almost geometrical form of the hat, and the base constituted by the line continuing from the left arm to the right hand, enclose the image with a rigor of style which is conscious. Every detail obeys that rigor. Consider the representation of the fur: the touches of light assume a regular, almost geometrical form. Thus light and shade do not stop at the surface of the image, but penetrate into its structure, offering the colors a prismatic form whence they shine forth.

This visualization is perhaps the source of the magic power of Vermeer, and is at one with an ideal and moral conception of the world.

54 · JAN VERMEER

Delft, born 1632, died 1675

YOUNG WOMAN WITH A WATER JUG

Canvas. Height 18 in.; width 16 in.

METROPOLITAN MUSEUM OF ART, NEW YORK

From the collection of Lord Powerscourt this painting came to Henry Marquand of New York and from him to the Metropolitan. It is a typical genre scene, and it allows us to understand the meaning of Vermeer's art, after the Young Girl with a Flute (No. 53) gave us the opportunity of analyzing his color and form.

To understand the development of Vermeer's style his few dated pictures are important. The Courtesan at Dresden is dated 1656, the Toilet of Diana at the Hague was also painted within the 'fifties. Neither represents the mature style of Vermeer. The Courtesan shows a certain vulgarity, common to the Dutch genre scenes but unknown to Vermeer's later style, and the Toilet of Diana shows ideal forms under Italian influence. Moreover, as has been pointed out, the composition of Christ at the house of Mary and Martha (Coats Collection, Skalmorlie Castle) was inspired by a painting by Alessandro Allori (Vienna Museum).

By contrast with these the two paintings representing a Geographer which are of 1665 (Gimpel Collection) and 1668 (Frankfort Museum) both show Vermeer's style in its full maturity and perfection.

Thus during the 'fifties Vermeer oscillated between the usual genre scene of his countrymen and the ideal forms of the Italians. During the 'sixties he achieved the synthesis of these, and created something new, unexpected and miraculous, his own art.

The Young Woman with a Water Jug is a perfect example of Vermeer scenes of the 'sixties. The young woman opens a window; she holds a brass jug in a basin on a table covered with an oriental rug. On the same table is an open jewel box. Against the wall is a leather chair with a blue drapery and a map. All this does not involve anything but the portrayal of a moment of everyday life. The preciousness of colors and the delicacy of half lights are so miraculous that they absorb the attention of the spectator, who has some difficulty in looking at anything else.

Certain forms, however, are impressive: the curve of the whitish blue collar over the elbows, rhythmically continued, even though narrowing, in the contours of the skirt; the cylindric purity of the arms, the discreet foreshortening of the whole figure, which reveals at once surface and depth. The same style can be seen in the smallest details, in the lights, reflections, and shadows of the basin and the jug, which have forms well adapted to an ideal architecture. This implies a longing for monumental qualities, for regular geometrical forms, for spiritual values which go far beyond any genre scene. Nothing is to be seen which could not be recognized as purely Dutch. Yet under the surface is an experience of the human dignity and the spiritual ideals proper to the Renaissance, which Vermeer's contemporaries had readily forgotten.

Vermeer was not only a discoverer of rare unknown harmonies of color, he was a man who was completely stranger to the materialism and vulgarity of the life of his time. He was gentle and delicate; he felt humility before anything in nature. With a touching naïveté he saw paradise on earth. Thus when he painted what he saw with natural power, with accuracy, with absolutely good faith that he was painting reality as it is, he painted a wonderful dream, the purest, the most enchanting of all dreams. He was an optimist who inspirited mankind by his vision. The very source of his poetry is his optimism. Today we praise his ability to offer his dreams with the illusion of their being reality; his contemporaries did not understand him because the world in which he lived was too ideal for them.

55 · JACOB VAN RUISDAEL

Haarlem, born 1628/9, died 1682

WHEATFIELDS

Canvas. Height 39⅜ in.; width 54¼ in.

ALTMAN COLLECTION. METROPOLITAN MUSEUM OF ART, NEW YORK

Through the collections of Comte de Colbert-La Pace and of Maurice Kann, this work, signed J V Ruisdael, came to that of Benjamin Altman, and through his bequest to the Metropolitan in 1913.

It is a picture quite famous among the works of Ruisdael, of his late period, when he took up again with enlarged vision and a greater mastery some of his early motifs. After the year 1650, his pictorial space was extended on the surface as well as in depth, that is, he composed with a formal theory which he learned under the influence of the Italianate Dutch artists just arrived from Italy, such as Jan Both. It may be that the panoramas of Philip Konincks also influenced Ruisdael. The new type of composition permitted Ruisdael's paintings to have a stronger unity and to fill the whole surface with a perfect coherence.

In his Wheatfields the pattern is clear. From a point in the road in the middle ground horizontal lines depart in all directions, suggesting a perspective, which alone works in the sky. The skies of Ruisdael are famous because they are not a background but a living whole, where the clouds, distant at the horizon, approach the spectator in the upper part, suggesting the concavity of the atmosphere. They are the necessary counterpart of the perspective ground.

Jacob van Ruisdael covered varied sorts of subject matter in his landscapes and showed different ideals, from the dramatic to the objectively realistic. But, as it has been noted, he avoided the too sentimental moments of nature, such as sunrises and sunsets, or the declines of nature in autumn or winter. His preference was for late spring and summer effects. The reason of this preference must be found in his gravity, his seriousness, in his moral restraint, which did not allow him to profit by the more superficially interesting aspects of nature. He was a physician, and belonged to the sect of Mennonites, one of the most spiritual among the sects of the Reformation.

The perspective structure of his landscapes and his moral earnestness permit us to interpret his attitude towards nature. If one compares his pictures with those of Claude Lorrain or of Italian landscapists, it would seem that Ruisdael lets nature speak for itself. If we take Dutch predecessors into consideration, men such as Jan van Goyen or Rembrandt, it appears that Ruisdael, while enriching the variety and the vitality of coloring, avoids any flight of fancy. Thus during the XIX century Ruisdael was exalted as the founder of the realistic style in landscape painting, the painter who was distinguished by his objective representation.

A truer insight reveals that his representation is nevertheless subjective. It is submitted to an imaginative composition, a subordination of all elements to a unique structure of light and shade, an exclusion of the interference of man in the majesty of nature. By so doing Ruisdael impressed upon all the trees and roads and fields and clouds his consciousness of the life of nature, even its dramatic life. The various elements which appear natural are parts of the whole. It is the whole that is subjective, connected with the baroque Dutch style, and clearly individual. This is the art of Ruisdael.

124

56 · MEINDERT HOBBEMA

Amsterdam, born 1638, died 1709

THE WATER MILL, "THE TREVOR LANDSCAPE"

Canvas. Height 38⅜ in.; width 56⅛ in.

JOHN HERRON ART INSTITUTE, INDIANAPOLIS

This painting, which is fully signed and dated 1667, was recorded in the collection of Lord Trevor in 1783. Thence it passed through the collections of Lady Hampden, John Walter, Sir Edgar Vincent, Viscount Esher and J. Pierpont Morgan, and finally was bought by the John Herron Art Institute in 1944. It was engraved by Richard Earlom (1742/3-1822), which illustrates its long renown.

Hobbema became a citizen of Amsterdam in 1659 and came under the influence of Ruisdael. He was very poorly paid for his pictures, and when, on his marriage in 1668, he secured a small post as a customs officer, he almost abandoned painting. In the years from 1663 to 1668 he had created a series of landscapes which are considered his masterpieces. Early in the XIX century this almost forgotten artist was again recognized — his paintings entered the greatest museums and collections, and he was even preferred to Ruisdael.

We see that he was a modest, practical man, without the grandeur of character which could persist and triumph over every obstacle. His tendency, his choice of motifs, stem from Ruisdael, but he lacks the imagination, the deep feeling, the magic of his master. Instead of Ruisdael's poetry, his art was one of prose; a prose, however, of honesty and health, of strength and penetration.

His choice of motifs is quite narrow, and he repeats them with slight variation, but with small changes in the point of view which prevent the several examples of the same motif from having the character of replicas. A mill between isolated or grouped trees, a brook, a winding path with a few farm houses, are the prevailing elements. Unlike Ruisdael, who prefers to show us nature undisturbed, Hobbema rarely omits the work of man. His is a workaday world. His strength lies in the grand lines carried through the picture, with the light falling in the middle ground between the trees, from which we penetrate into the depths or can move in many directions. His execution is accurate, accomplished, observant of details, without being warm or enlivening.

Looking at the Trevor Landscape, one feels an invitation to enter into the picture and walk about the water and the mill, through the grounds, under the trees, in order to participate in the simple life of the woman with the cow and of the two peasants, father and son. One believes in the goodness of heart of the painter, who presents for contemplation not only a pleasant scene of nature but some fine lights and delicate trees and foliage.

Modern criticism, when taste has changed so much from that of the middle of the XIX century, finds more observation than creativity in the style of Hobbema. His good faith, his love of nature, and the seriousness of his effort to give pleasure to mankind are the mainsprings of his art.

57 · NICOLAS POUSSIN

Villères (Andelys), born 1593/4, died 1665

THE TRIUMPH OF NEPTUNE AND AMPHITRITE

Canvas. Height 42½ in.; width 75½ in.

GEORGE W. ELKINS COLLECTION. PHILADELPHIA MUSEUM OF ART, PHILADELPHIA

Gian Pietro Bellori, the first biographer of Poussin, tells that, besides four bacchanals, he painted for Cardinal Richelieu, "a triumph of Neptune on the sea, in his car, drawn by sea horses, followed by fanciful Tritons and Nereids." It was executed in Rome between 1638 and 1640. After having belonged to the Fromont de Brevanne, Boyer d'Aguilles and Crozat collections, it was acquired by Catherine II in 1772 for the Hermitage, Leningrad. There in 1932 it was purchased for the Philadelphia Museum of Art.

Amphitrite became the wife of Neptune, and in antique reliefs they are represented together in a chariot, with the idea of deifying them both. Poussin's idea is likewise an apotheosis rather than a triumph, as we conceive one today. As a drawing in the Stockholm Museum shows that his first thought was to paint a Triumph of Galatea, the change was perhaps so as to be freer from Raphael's Galatea, from which, however, he borrowed the figure of the Triton behind Neptune.

The period between 1635 to 1650 is considered the one of maturity and perfection in Poussin's art. In 1624 he had settled in Rome, and had developed the style of XVII century "classicism" in painting, of which he is the outstanding representative.

The enthusiasm for the antique, either its myths or its forms, is the basis of classicism. It had been created by Raphael, in Rome, more than a century before Poussin and it continued through the "mannerists," the Carracci, Guido Reni, Domenichino and so on. But mannerism had accustomed artists to an ease of execution which had encouraged painters to be quick and superficial in the pursuit of their classic ideal. The result was pleasant and rich decoration rather than really creative art.

Poussin had a difficult character, which contrasted with the pliability of these painters. He was rude and sharp, he felt very strongly his independence and his originality. Thus he refused to become a decorative painter, even when the king of France desired him to do so, and kept straight to his own aim.

His artistic reticence was parallel to his moral reserve. Everybody knows the excesses of baroque painting, which were flights of fancy without control. Poussin always checked his fancy through the theory of "reason," with a severity unknown to the XVII century Italians. No one can define what is meant by reason in art, but for Poussin reason was a measure, a restraint, against excesses of any kind. Thus he was called the painter philosopher. Critics have vainly tried to find his philosophy in the themes of his subject matter. His philosophy consists in his restraint. With restraint alone, however, he could not make a work of art; his creative imagination had to enjoy a certain freedom. Pagan mythology, ideal beauty, satisfaction in images of nobility, and above all ecstasy before scenes of landscape, inspired Poussin's masterpieces.

He drew on several sources of inspiration in order to build up a scene like that of the theatre. Dufresnoy said that painting is the sister of tragedy; Félibien, the friend of Poussin, said that his pictures were painted according to the rules of theatrical writing. In fact, the content of the Triumph of Neptune and Amphitrite is a theatrical apotheosis. One is bound to admire the order of the composition, where figures are in motion, and draperies are floating in the air, but the movement, which makes the scene alive, depends on a subtle balance. In the XVII century no one believed in the myth of Neptune and Amphitrite, but Poussin found satisfaction in recalling the antique myths and gave pleasure to his contemporaries as well as to posterity. In the horses and in the landscape he went beyond his own classic ideal. There his poetical feeling finds an energy which raises the apotheosis towards an ideal life, where all artificiality is excluded in an atmosphere of pure art.

58 · GIAN BATTISTA TIEPOLO

Venice, born 1696, died 1770

Armida Abandoned by Rinaldo

Canvas. Height 73½ in.; width 102 in.

ART INSTITUTE OF CHICAGO, CHICAGO

This painting, together with three other canvases also in the Chicago Art Institute, constituted a decoration painted by Tiepolo for Count Serbelloni of Milan. They illustrate the story of the love of Rinaldo and Armida as narrated by Torquato Tasso in Cantos XIV, XVI and XVII of his *Jerusalem Delivered*. From Count Serbelloni the four paintings passed to the Cartier collection in Genoa, then to the Deering collection, Chicago. They were bequeathed by Mr. Deering to the Art Institute.

The scene of Armida abandoned by Rinaldo is inspired by the following verses of Tasso, as translated by Sir John K. James:

> While she came up all breathless and dissolved in tears;
> And tho' in greater grief she could not be,
> Still not more sad than lovely she appears.
> She looks—she looks him thro'—yet speaketh naught:
> Or that she scorns, or thinks, or does not dare.
> He durst not look; and if a look he caught,
> 'Twas with a furtive self-reproachful air.

Tiepolo enjoyed painting the legend of Rinaldo, which he did repeatedly: in the frescoes at the Villa Valmarana near Vicenza (1737), in those of the Castle of Würzburg (1751-1753), and in a sketch for a Würzburg scene in the Berlin Museum. The Chicago series, of which Gian Battista's authorship is confirmed by an engraving by his son, Lorenzo Tiepolo, must be dated between 1737 and 1751. The figures of the Chicago series are later than the Valmarana paintings because there is less contrast of light and shade, and they precede the Würzburg ones because their forms are less broken and rapid.

Tiepolo plays with fancy, without any interest in physical or psychological reality. In the XVIII century the theatre dominated the world of art and offered a substitute for reality by suggesting subject matter to painters. In Tiepolo's picture Rinaldo is a pleasing angel, but he is not "self-reproachful," Armida is "lovely" but not very sad. Both play a sweet comedy, like those of Metastasio. So too with the armor, the tree, or the column; they belong to the costumes and scenes of the theatre.

In spite of this, Tiepolo is today considered a great painter, after a long eclipse which lasted from about 1800 to 1880. Oblivion and praise depend on the importance given to the subject matter. If one takes the abandonment of Armida by Rinaldo seriously, one will be shocked by the lack of human tragedy in Tiepolo's painting; if, in the painting of a tree, one wishes to see the real tree, one will be shocked by the canvas tree of Tiepolo.

But the ways to reach art are infinite. The subject matter is only a pretext for Tiepolo. His motif is a theatrical fancy, and it is the motif, not the subject matter, which is the real content of a work of art. The critical problem is to understand if the form created by the artist is perfectly coherent with his own motif, whatever it may be.

From this point of view Tiepolo's painting is a masterpiece. The form is broken enough to avoid any academic conventionality, while it creates a new conventionality. Academic conventionality is not art because it is learned and repeated, the new one is art because it is created. However the form of the images is only a pretext for coloring. It is Tiepolo's coloring which is the masterpiece, and which is unique. The use of neutral colors to enhance the brilliancy of yellows, pinks, sky blues and so on, is entirely personal. It has been said that for the revival of coloring, attenuated by the luministic style of the XVII century, Tiepolo was inspired by Paolo Veronese. But Tiepolo's color has nothing to do with Veronese's. His color harmony is broken as are his forms. Thus new accents of color appear which are fresh and arouse a new ecstasy.

Only a lazy and idle society, without contact with the realities of life, could provide the environment for such a painting. The price paid was the French Revolution. But we have sufficient historical sense to appreciate a creative genius even if produced by a society of that kind.

59 · FRANCESCO GUARDI

Venice, born 1712, died 1793

THE CANNAREGIO AND THE THREE ARCHED BRIDGE

Canvas. Height 18¾ in.; width 29¼ in.

A good example of the mature and late style of the artist is this painting, which belonged to the Chiesa collection, Milan.

The Cannaregio is the largest canal connecting the Grand Canal with the lagoon, a traffic channel quite distant from the monumental zone, and seldom visited by lovers of Venice. Why did Guardi choose this remote canal as the subject of one of his masterpieces? The reason is to be found in the Three Arched Bridge. Its form is a combination of straight and curved lines, of surfaces interrupted by reinforcements, niches and tablets adorned with sculptured reliefs. The whole has a rhythm of the dance. Nothing could better suggest the rococo style.

The style of Guardi, indeed, is related to an ideal dance. Even the effects of light and shade on the buildings seem to participate in a rhythm, together with the sketched figures of his gondoliers and with the reflections in the water. During the XVII century contrasts of straight and curved lines and of lights and shadows had been specially created in order to attain an emphasis on monumentality, power, and energy. Guardi is too skeptical and too modest to emphasize anything himself, and uses the contrasts which had been created for emphasis in the bridge, without any emphasis of his own, just for the pleasure of variety and fancy. The same change took place when the baroque style became the rococo in architecture and decoration.

Something was lost, but a new finesse arose, favorable to creative freedom. First of all art was released from any subjection to propaganda, either political or religious, and was brought to the level of every day life. Some buildings, a canal, a few boats, a bridge—these are the components of this picture. They seem assembled in a casual way, but are not, because they respond to a necessity of style. That is, by lowering the ideal of art, some painters (and Guardi is by far the best of them) made their ideal come true.

The XVIII century discovered the "picturesque," that is, an ideal which could not identify itself with beauty, but was attractive enough because it was proper to painting. Before the picturesque there had been the "pictorial," that is, a style of painting where the exigencies of colors, lights and shadows predominated over those of plastic form. The picturesque was the projection into nature of what had been discovered in the pictorial. It was a pretext for pictorial style, but not an artistic style in itself. The greatness of Guardi as an artist consists in his ability to transform the picturesque in his pictorial style, to let his motif and his form coincide.

The pictorial style had been developed in the painting of human figures, and Guardi had the advantage of being educated in a family of painters of religious scenes. His elder contemporary, Canaletto, in spite of his greatness, did not transform his views of Venice into a purely pictorial style. To do so a lack of severity, of faithfulness to reality, was necessary. With the help of genius and of his own shortcomings Guardi was able to create his lasting vision of a rococo Venice.

60 · ANTOINE WATTEAU

Valenciennes, born 1684, died 1721

THE FRENCH COMEDIANS

Canvas. Height 22½ in.; width 28¾ in.

Watteau's patron, Jean de Julienne, was the first owner of this painting. Through Count von Rothenburg, Prussian Ambassador to France, it was acquired by Frederick the Great, and remained at the palace in Potsdam, near Berlin, until it was sold to Mr. Jules S. Bache.

It is a grouping of actors, representing on the left Tragedy, with the characters of *L'Amant*, *L'Amante*, and *La Confidante*, and on the right Comedy with the parts of *Matamore* and *Crispin*. M. Couet, Librarian of the Comédie Française, thought that these images of actors were portraits, particularly of Mlle. Duclos and M. Beaubourg, in the two figures standing in the foreground, and of Paul Poisson in the Crispin mounting the stairs.

Between Poussin and Watteau two events of importance had taken place in the field of taste. One was the controversy between the supporters of Poussin and those of Rubens. The former were for classic design, imitation of the antique and the rhetorical taste called "le grand goût," the latter, for brilliancy of color, modern feeling and natural truth. The second event was the *Querelle des Anciens et des Modernes*, which questioned the value of technical science and perfection, in favor of spontaneity in art.

Watteau was enthusiastic for Rubens, the Flemish genre painters and the Venetians. By his work he destroyed the rhetorical tradition of the French Academy, the false heroics of common baroque painting, and went back to the representation of life. In his early days he wanted to paint the every day life of peasants and soldiers, but later he found a reality of his own, better suited to his poetic dream.

Here the choice of actors as subject matter is of great importance. A comedian is a reality, a man or a woman, but he is also an artistic image, insofar as he represents a part. In this painting Poisson is the man Poisson, but he is also Crispin, the artistic phantasm. Watteau saw in an actor the necessary mediator between nature and art. By painting actors he abandoned rhetoric and reached reality, but a reality which had in itself an aspect of art. The imagination of the painter could develop more freely, because in the subject matter itself there was a large element of fancy. The connection between the form of Watteau and the subject matter of comedians was such that all his figures appear as figures of an ideal comedy. The subject matter had become a *style*.

On the stage, love was the main motif, and in XVIII century Paris love acquired a special character of *esprit*, finesse and gallantry. From this point of view, the painting of Watteau at the very beginning of the century proclaimed the trend of mind of the Louis XV era. On the other hand, the influence of Rubens and the Venetians tied Watteau to XVIIth century tradition. The elegant love of the XVIII century is represented by Watteau with a deep sensuousness which still belongs to XVII century realism. Hence the unique power of vitality underlining his grace, his energy of form and color, which evaporates in a light fancy.

As a man, Watteau was poor in health, melancholy and caustic: "intellectually a libertine but morally a wise man" said his friend Gersaint. Behind his fanciful scenes, his *fêtes galantes*, there is a real love, free of constraint, in a paradise on earth which existed in fact, but only in his paintings.

61 · FRANÇOIS BOUCHER

Paris, born 1703, died 1770

THE AMUSEMENTS OF WINTER

Canvas. Height 22 in.; width 28 in.

Boucher painted this picture for Madame de Pompadour together with three others representing Spring, Summer and Autumn, thus forming an ensemble of the four seasons. These were inherited by Madame de Pompadour's brother, the Marquis de Marigny. Subsequently they passed through the Beaujon, Vernier, and Ridgway collections in Paris, and that of Mr. and Mrs. Edward Bacon in New York. In 1916 they were acquired for the Frick Collection.

The Four Seasons was a theme treated by artists even in the Middle Ages, but it must be noted that the accent of Boucher's series is on pleasure, as indicated by the titles of engravings by Jean Daullé: The Charms of Spring, The Pleasures of Summer, The Delights of Autumn, The Amusements of Winter. Thus the seasons and the world are only a pretext for decoration, for amusement, and fondness for pretty girls. This is typical, for Boucher is a representative of the era of Louis XV.

The style of Boucher does not derive from a revolution in pictorial taste, as does that of Watteau, but from a change in decorative taste. Between 1730 and 1731 had appeared the "genre pittoresque," characterized by asymmetry and contrasts. Created chiefly by the goldsmith Oppenord and the sculptor Nicolas Pineau, it was the second and final phase of the rococo style. In painting François Boucher represents this new trend of taste in the most brilliant way.

He had the greatest of success, winning the grand prize of the Academy at twenty and becoming a member of it at twenty-eight. He provided designs for tapestries of Beauvais and of the Gobelins, for porcelain of Vincennes and Sèvres, and for the illustrations of books. His production is immense. It is characterized by a spicy verve and an incredible ease.

His form is pleasant without any rigor; it is as superficial as is his expression of grace, as conventional as his color. In short he is not a painter of life, but a painter of the *salon*, that is of the conventional life of the upper classes of the XVIII century which was destroyed by the French Revolution. Thus he was an appropriate mirror of a moment of taste, rather than a real creator of taste.

His verve succeeds in achieving creation when he escapes from his conventions, for example in certain landscapes. In The Amusements of Winter the snowy landscape has a delicacy of color and simplicity of form which is lacking in the figures.

63 · JEAN HONORÉ FRAGONARD

Grasse, born 1732, died 1806

THE BILLET DOUX (THE LOVE LETTER)

Canvas. Height 32¾ in.; width 26⅜ in.

BACHE COLLECTION. METROPOLITAN MUSEUM OF ART, NEW YORK

This painting was formerly in the collections of Baron Feuillet de Conches, Madame Jäger-Schmidt, Ernest Cronier, and Ernest Bardac. It ultimately became part of the collection of Mr. Jules S. Bache, which was placed in the Metropolitan Museum of Art.

The love letter which gives the title to the painting bears the name of M. Cuvilier. Charles-Etienne-Gabriel Cuvilier was an officer of the buildings of the Crown from 1764 on and was acquainted with the painter François Boucher. The second daughter of the latter, Marie Emilie, born in 1740, who had married the painter Baudouin and become a widow in 1769, married M. Cuvilier in 1773. Fragonard, who had been a pupil of Boucher, painted her portrait with a graceful and benevolent malice as revealing her love affair. The probable date of the painting is therefore 1771 or 1772.

Pupil of Boucher, Fragonard is as light and libertine as his master. But he has a completely different temperament. Above all, he is a born painter and a poet. He employs all the conventionalities of the time, but under his brush, they become creative fancies. His subject matter is often more erotic than that of Boucher, but the verve, the youthfulness and the fancy of Fragonard transfer all the ambiguous themes to a level where the creative imagination dominates.

His impulse to paint love and nothing else is also a reaction against a new trend of taste, the dawn of neo-classicism. When Fragonard went back to Paris after his Italian years he found the new taste affirmed. He painted Corésus and Callirhoe, (now at the Louvre), a huge academic canvas, in order to please the critics and officialdom, and to be accepted by the Academy. He achieved great success, but he must have felt that the academic style was opposed to his artistic temperament. The fact is that he soon renounced academic glory as well as royal orders so as to please the libertines, the financiers, the actresses and the dancers. Thus his dedication to the frivolous themes assumed an aspect of protest which necessarily influenced his style.

One of the fundamental requirements of any academy is diligent finishing in painting. Fragonard could finish but he did not want to do it. His verve called for a finish of its own, a suggestion of quickness and lightness of touch equal to the lightness of his imagination. To achieve this a polemical attitude was necessary, which was lacking in Boucher.

Fragonard was a Southerner, he had a hot temper, a lack of reserve, a youthful sprightliness. His vivid imagination went far beyond his natural sensuality. Images in perennial movement, a sketchy and improvised execution, the imprint of love even in the atmosphere, a coloring which is not rich but full of nuances and suggestions, finally an extreme elegance given to any painted object—these are some of the components of his style.

The Billet Doux could not be more charming and graceful or more full of humor. But these qualities, which are almost too apparent, cannot veil the creative spirit of a real painter, who manifests himself in the vibration of his light and color.

64 · WILLIAM HOGARTH

London, born 1679, died 1764

THE LADY'S LAST STAKE

Canvas. Height 36 in.; width 41½ in.

ALBRIGHT ART GALLERY, BUFFALO. SEYMOUR H. KNOX FUND

This satire was painted by Hogarth for Lord Charlemont in 1759. It remained in the Charlemont family until 1874 when it was sold at Christie's. Then it belonged to the collections of Louis Huth and of J. Pierpont Morgan. Another version of the picture is in the collection of the Duke of Richmond.

Hogarth himself wrote about this picture: "When I was making arrangements to confine myself entirely to my graver, an amiable nobleman (Lord Charlemont) requested that before I bade final adieu to the pencil, I would paint him one picture. The subject to be my own choice, and the reward whatever I demanded. The story I pitched upon was a young and virtuous married lady, who by playing cards with an officer, loses her money, watch and jewels; the moment when he offers them back in return for her honor, and she is wavering at his suit, was my point of time."

Miss Hester Lynch Salusbury, afterwards the famous Mrs. Thrale of Samuel Johnson's circle, and still later Mrs. Piozzi, claimed to have sat for the lady in this picture. The scene is the interior of a room, painted, it is believed, from a chamber in Hogarth's country box at Chiswick. The time, indicated by a clock on the mantel-piece of the room, is five minutes to five on a bright morning, dawn is seen through the uncurtained window, the nearly burnt-out candles attached to a picture over the fireplace attest how long the pair have been gambling.

In 1758, when Hogarth painted The Lady's Last Stake, he had failed in his second attempt at a career as a portrait painter. His success as a painter of moral comedies was over, and his polemical hostility to the fashionable society of his time was stronger than ever. Hogarth himself tells us: "I have endeavored to treat my subjects as a dramatic writer; my picture is my stage, and men and women my players, who by means of certain actions and gestures, are to exhibit a dumb show." From this point of view The Lady's Last Stake is fully successful. The details of the scene make the dramatic moment clear. Moreover, the false innocence of the officer's gesture and the thoughtful glance of the lady at her own wavering, have a humorous wit which is reminiscent of a good writer of comedy. Today everybody knows that this is the illustrative aspect of a painting—a secondary quality in art. Many Dutch painters, as well as Watteau and his followers, so diffused this quality in the whole of Europe, that it renders this painting a good document of the taste of the time.

But if we wish to know what there is in Hogarth that pertains to real art as we think of it today, we must recall another passage from Hogarth himself, relative to his purpose in his *Four Stages of Cruelty*. "The leading points in these, as well as the two preceding prints, were made as obvious as possible, in the hope that their tendency might be seen by men of the lowest rank. Neither minute accuracy of design, nor fine engraving, was deemed necessary. . . . The passions may be more forcibly expressed by a strong bold stroke, than by the most delicate engraving."

Hogarth followed his aesthetics. He wanted forcibly to express passions and he improvised images without too much care for delicacy of painting. The painting of his day was too artificial and conventional. Hogarth's devotion to an "inferior" branch, genre painting, and his bold strokes allowed him to brave the aesthetic prejudices of his time. Thus his crusade as a moralist and his urge for polemics undoubtedly resulted in some benefits to art and taste.

The brilliancy of his images depends on his "serpentine" contour lines, which suggest movement and therefore life. It is still a superficial life, tied to the subject matter rather than to a visual coherence, but it well corresponds to that taste which has been called the "picturesque rococo."

65 · SIR JOSHUA REYNOLDS

Plympton (Devonshire), born 1723, died 1792

LADY CAROLINE HOWARD

Canvas. Height 56¼ in.; width 44½ in.

MELLON COLLECTION. NATIONAL GALLERY OF ART, WASHINGTON

This portrait was painted about 1778, and was engraved in that very year by Valentine Green. One year later it was exhibited at the Royal Academy. Formerly in the possession of Frederick Howard, 5th Earl of Carlisle it descended to the Hon. Geoffrey William Algernon Howard, fifth son of the 9th Earl, of Castle Howard, Yorkshire.

Modern criticism has been very severe on Reynolds. It has made light of his academic *Discourses*, has emphasized the unattractive sides of his personality ("an arrivist, a humbug and a snob"), and has denied him any spontaneity of creation. No doubt his strength of will was responsible for his determination to become a successful artist in order to convince himself that he was also a great artist. But he knew that he was not; the concentration of his effort which, in a way, served as a substitute for free creativity, made him a pathetic character in spite of all his successes.

The portrait of Lady Caroline Howard shows an attractive child, seven years old, seated in a landscape before a big pot of roses. She is richly dressed; her attitude in picking a rose is one of dignity. It is a portrait for show, stressing the nobility and well being of the child's family.

It was Van Dyck who gave portraiture a social aspect and made it fashionable to show the class of the sitter rather than his individual character. Reynolds went farther because he believed that a portrait might give grace, likeness and "general air" instead of individuality. He painted the face of the sitter from life in a few hours, he then supplied the face a suitable costume and setting. Roger Fry wrote: "When we think of the distinction of English society in the eighteenth century, of its special note of easy simplicity of manner, its unaffected and unconscious dignity, its discretion, it is round Reynolds' portraits that our imagination crystallizes."

It is a further merit of Reynolds that he had so catholic a taste that English painting was less affected by neo-classicism than the schools of painting on the Continent. He tried to harmonize all the different components of style he had drawn from Rome and Venice, from Antwerp and Amsterdam. This is of importance in the history of taste.

So far as art proper is concerned, one observes in the portrait of Lady Caroline Howard a pleasing flat image, a distinguished and cursory drawing, without any plastic energy, no visual connection between image and space. Reynolds wrote of painting: "The great end of the art is to strike the imagination." The detachment and the isolation of the image does indeed let the figure strike our imagination. But if we ask for something more, for what Reynolds felt before that charming child, we are disappointed.

Lady Caroline Howard
Lady Cawdor.

66 · THOMAS GAINSBOROUGH

Sudbury, born 1727, died 1788

THE BLUE BOY

Canvas. Height 70 in.; width 48 in.

Gainsborough painted this portrait about 1769-1770. It represents Jonathan Buttall, son of John Buttall, an ironmonger who had a prosperous business at Soho in London. Jonathan carried on the family business until 1796, when his effects as well as "capital pictures and drawings by Gainsborough" were sold. He died in London in 1805. From the Buttall family the painting passed to John Nesbitt, M. P., John Hopper, R.A., Earl Grosvenor and the Duke of Westminster, Grosvenor House, London.

The x-ray has proved that the Blue Boy was painted on a canvas where the painter had begun a full length portrait, and which was larger than it is now. The comparatively thick pigment used is probably accounted for by Gainsborough's intention to conceal the painting underneath. This also suggests that the portrait of Buttall was improvised.

The Van Dyck costume was used in other paintings by Gainsborough, and thus doubtless belonged to the painter. It is possible that he lent it to the boy for a social function, was struck with his appearance in it, and took the first canvas at his disposal in order to capture this.

The Blue Boy is commonly, and probably rightly, believed to be *the* masterpiece of Gainsborough. It is interesting to reflect on its origins—the portrait of a young friend, dressed in sumptuous but amusing garments, as in a masquerade, improvised on an old canvas to preserve an impression of vitality, youthfulness and glamour. The blue of the costume, the dominant note and the reason for the famous name of the picture, the simplicity of the pose was due to the spontaneity of the endeavour; the thickness of the pigment was the result of the necessity of concealing the previous painting. All this seems to indicate a casual way of painting, but the real masterpiece often depends upon genius overcoming pure chance, on his struggle against material difficulties.

At its first appearance at the Royal Academy in 1770 the Blue Boy produced a sensation. Mary Moser wrote to Fuseli: "Gainsborough is beyond himself in a portrait of a gentleman in a Vandyke habit." In 1832 the old artist, John Taylor, then in his ninety-third year, recollected that his master Hayman had told him "What an extraordinary picture Gainsborough had painted of the Blue Boy; it is as fine as Vandyke." When the painting was bought by Mr. Huntington from the Duke of Westminster in 1922, and was exhibited at the National Gallery in London before crossing the ocean, within three weeks more than 90,000 people went to pay it their sad farewell.

A painting of such wide renown has been explained by a theoretical contrast between Gainsborough and Reynolds, who had denied that a fine painting could be obtained by a predominant note of blue. Today we know that the Blue Boy did not originate in an academic controversy; the rhetorical hint was in the legend, not in the picture.

The painting has its exceptional value because of the intensity of Gainsborough's vitality, of his sense of individuality, of the rhythm of his form, and of the perfectly spontaneous coherence between his impression and his image. Above all it is his poetry which transforms life into a vibrating image, parallel to but higher than life itself. Gainsborough was a landscapist, in his human figures he concentrated what he had felt in the whole of nature besides what he had known from a great tradition of culture. A happy moment, that of the Blue Boy. Heaven and earth met to pay him their homage.

67 · GEORGE ROMNEY

Dalton in Furness, born 1734, died 1802

MRS. DAVENPORT

Canvas. Height 30 in.; width 25 in.

The sittings for this portrait are recorded in Romney's diaries during the years 1782-1784. John Jones engraved it in 1784.

Charlotte Davenport, born in 1756, was the daughter of Ralph Sneyd of Keele Hall, Newcastle-under-Lyme, Staffordshire. In 1777 she married Davies Davenport, High Sheriff of Cheshire, and Member of Parliament for that county from 1806 to 1830. From the family of Davies Davenport, Capesthorne, Cheshire, the portrait was inherited by Sir William Bromley-Davenport, Chelford, Cheshire, who sold the painting to Mr. Mellon.

Romney was only seven years younger than Gainsborough, but his art belongs to a different world. The tradition of the Venetians and of Van Dyck no longer counts for him. Reynolds, in spite of his academic taste had avoided neo-classicism, and had mediated between the baroque past and the romantic future. Romney, on the other hand, became the standard bearer of neo-classic portrait painting in England. On the continent neo-classicism was a reaction against baroque and rococo both for aesthetic and social purposes. Romney was still tied to the social habits of the eighteenth century, thus his adoption of neo-classicism was limited to aesthetic motives.

Color had been the principal interest of Reynolds and Gainsborough. Romney appears quite indifferent to color, he spreads tints on flat zones like the tones of a map. These tints are charming, but they seldom reach that life which transforms tints into color.

His artistic accent is on line. His drawing is simplified and easy, aiming at likeness and at superficial grace. Ease and grace are characteristic of his work; above all in his portraits of women there is an attractiveness which is his poetry.

The portrait of Mrs. Davenport is one of his happiest achievements, and reveals not only the charm of the young lady but a special style which pertains both to the sitter and the painter. It is the simplicity, the elegance and the reserve of English gentry at the end of the eighteenth century. As a document of a way of social life, on a very high plane, this painting is notable.

In accordance with the taste of the time, Romney wanted to be a painter of history. It was only his success as a portrait painter which obliged him to represent the belles of London society. A relation exists between this success and his indifference towards the most profound problems of form and color. He had learned in France and Italy, where he worked between 1773 and 1775, what classic art was, but he never became a pedantic classicist. The buoyancy of his feeling and the natural elegance of his nature favoured his success, more than did the endeavour of more gifted artists.

68 · JOHN SINGLETON COPLEY

Boston, born 1738, died 1815

PORTRAIT OF JOSHUA HENSHAW

Canvas. Height 49¾ in.; width 39¾ in.

CALIFORNIA PALACE OF THE LEGION OF HONOR, SAN FRANCISCO

This portrait belonged in 1873 to Dr. J. McLean Hayward of Boston, a great grand-nephew of the sitter. From the Hayward family it went to the California Palace of the Legion of Honor.

Joshua Henshaw (1703-1777) of Boston, a merchant and a magistrate, was a distinguished patriot and a member of the House of Representatives. Together with John Hancock, James Otis and Samuel Adams, he protested invasion of the rights of the colonies and was forced in 1774 to flee from Boston and take refuge in Leicester, Massachusetts.

This painting is considered to date from 1770 to 1774, that is, it belongs to the last American period of Copley. He left for Europe in June, 1774, settled in London and never returned to America. In London he had exhibited portraits long before his removal to England. When he settled there he sought renown through historical pictures following the fashion of the time. At first he succeeded, but later his good fortune decreased. There is no doubt that Copley's best achievements are his portraits before 1774, when he was little cultivated and provincial, but worked seriously with great care and persistence.

His motive in painting was to obtain a likeness, which is not itself an artistic aim, at least in the opinion of our time. In his earliest period the likeness was approximate, generalized, materialized, with poor drawing, with dull color, without life. But in his portraits after 1760 one sees that something is stirring in them, that some brush strokes determine an individual character, and impress life on the faces and the hands, finally that color becomes richer and sometimes precious. The portrait of Mrs. Nathaniel Appleton (Fogg Art Museum, Cambridge) shows that this enrichment of form and color has attained its full power and has brought the painter to the level of art.

Copley had been self taught, in spite of some influences from John Greenwood, Robert Feke and Joseph Blackburn. What he learned from them were formulae through which he could not reach art. But he was painstaking, and insisted. To fix a detail meant to give life to that extent. When he succeeded in finding an appropriate organization of his details, the result was good as painting, the forms and colors acquired a soul. The stronger the individualization of the sitter, the more fully his character and his moral expression were embodied.

When Copley portrayed Joshua Henshaw he found before him a man of great energy and character, one of those who began the Revolution. Copley understood this strength, painted this strength, and made one of his most natural portraits, where the characteristic succeeds in attaining life.

This advance from the generalized formulae of his early portraits to the living character of Joshua Henshaw is a development from the abstract to the concrete in painting, a development which is common to many artists who were trained in the academic tradition. But the achievement of Copley is that his training was very poor, that he reached his best production through a constant effort of observation, accurate execution and strength of character, which constitute his style.

69 · GILBERT STUART

Narragansett, Rhode Island, born 1755, died 1828

Mrs. Richard Yates

Canvas. Height 30¼ in.; width 25 in.

MELLON COLLECTION. NATIONAL GALLERY OF ART, WASHINGTON

This portrait came from the collections of Dr. Isaak M. Cline, New Orleans and Thomas B. Clarke, New York. It was painted in 1793, the very year of Stuart's return from Ireland to New York. Mrs. Yates was the wife of a New York merchant.

It is difficult to imagine a greater difference than between the careers of Copley and Stuart. The aim of both in painting was the likeness of the sitter. But Copley was self taught, and gradually reached his artistic level through constant efforts, until in Europe he deviated from the line of his natural gifts towards historical painting. He arrived in Europe and in a center of artistic culture at thirty-six years of age, and remained in England until his death. On the contrary Stuart went to England when twenty years old, became a pupil and a friend of Benjamin West, received the advice of Gainsborough, portrayed Sir Joshua Reynolds, discovered the talent of the young Thomas Lawrence, and mastered all the refinements of British painting at the end of the XVIII century. He had remarkable success, both as a painter and socially; he "emulated in style and costliness the leader of English fashion, the then Prince of Wales," as Dunlap says. His lavish mode of life was perhaps one of the reasons of his success, but was also the cause of his flight from London to Ireland, where he stayed from 1787 to 1793. Finally he returned to the United States, partly in order to paint portraits of Washington, which he believed he would sell in good quantity. He stayed in New York, Philadelphia and Washington until 1805, when he removed to Boston where he lived until his death. Portraiture was therefore the only form of his artistic activity. The "accuracy of similitude" was recognized in London as his great merit, even though in 1786 it was remarked that his portraits were "strong resemblances, but a set of more interesting vapid countenances it is not easy to imagine."

This criticism is vitiated by the prejudice in favor of a classical ideal, so widespread in 1786. But it is not entirely wrong, at least for the majority of Stuart's official portraits. Fortunately, that of Mrs. Richard Yates is not an official portrait and its simple likeness is sufficient to permit Stuart to find style in the individual character of the sitter. The faithfulness to the model excludes here any idea of beauty, that is, of emphasis, of idealizing, of official dignity. Mrs. Yates is sewing, she stops and looks at her painter, without any expression other than that of a life which is peaceful, monotonous and serene. Stuart, who in London and in Dublin was accustomed to wholly different models, was stirred by her appearance and his reaction was appropriate: even his coloring is subdued and his form has not the usual plastic quality. This deviation from his rhetoric, this spontaneous reaction and this truthfulness to his impression, resulted in a work of art which is rightly considered one of the best achievements of Stuart.

70 · FRANCISCO JOSÉ de GOYA y LUCIENTES

Fuendetodos, born 1746, died 1828

THE MARQUESA DE PONTEJOS

Canvas. Height 83 in.; width 49½ in.

MELLON COLLECTION. NATIONAL GALLERY OF ART, WASHINGTON

From the collection of the Marqués de Miraflores y de Pontejos, Madrid, this portrait came directly to the Mellon Collection.

It is one of the most outstanding examples of the art of Goya in his early maturity, between 1785 and 1790. It was the moment when Goya, of poor and provincial extraction, obtained the favour of the court and the aristocracy of Madrid. It was his moment of optimism. In 1784 he wrote that he was successful in the circle of intelligentsia and with the public at large. Two years later he wrote that, in spite of limited profits, he was satisfied as the happiest of men. By 1788 he was overburdened with commissions, and complained that he was unable to pursue his work with the necessary diligence. When, in 1791, he was denounced because he did not work for the manufactory of tapestries, the king supported him, entertained him with the malicious gossip against him, and played the violin for him.

The artistic experience of Goya had been very complex. He freed himself from the late Neapolitan baroque style through the influence of Mengs, Tiepolo and Velasquez. The secrets of the XVIII century concerning line, color and light were familiar to him. But when he became the favoured portraitist of the Spanish aristocracy he felt that English painting, and above all Gainsborough, could give him good suggestions. These concerned not only aristocratic taste, but also delicacy and grace of coloring.

In the portrait of the Marquesa de Pontejos, her relation to space, as well as her frontal pose, may have been inspired by English models. Her shepherdess costume, inspired by Marie Antoinette, is of French origin. The finesse of the contour lines and the immobility of the pose recall Mengs. The vague landscape of the background is similar to those Goya used in tapestries.

In spite of all these observations and reminiscences, the originality and the creative character of the portrait are clear and self-evident. The poetic touch of Goya consists in his fanciful transformation of the lady into a charming puppet, and of the portrait into a fairy tale.

Goya was of humble family. He was sound, passionate and naturally serious. He could not become a courtier, he could not believe in the frivolous life of the aristocracy and the court. Later he became a rebel, and engraved and painted what he himself called "monsters." But when he painted the Marquesa de Pontejos he was enjoying his success and was happy.

It was about this time that he fell in love with the Duchess of Alba, whom he likewise painted as an attractive puppet. The life of the aristocracy appeared to him as a fairy tale. He enjoyed it, but he was a stranger to it. It was this detachment which permitted him to see that the Marquesa was a figure of pure fancy and that his own fancy could coincide with it. The result was a unique masterpiece.

71 · FRANCISCO JOSÉ de GOYA y LUCIENTES

Fuendetodos, born 1746, died 1828

MAJAS ON A BALCONY

Canvas. Height 76¾ in.; width 49½ in.

HAVEMEYER COLLECTION. METROPOLITAN MUSEUM OF ART, NEW YORK

This painting formerly belonged to the Infante Don Sebastián Gabriel de Borbon y Braganza. It passed to the Duke of Marchena, Madrid, before becoming part of the Havemeyer Collection.

Two other versions of the subject exist, both in Paris. One, very similar to this, was in the Montpensier collection and later in that of Edmond de Rothschild; the other, considerably different, was formerly in the Salamanca collection and is now in the Groult collection. A fourth and smaller version, which was in the Galerie Espagnole in the Louvre in 1838, as a loan from Louis Philippe, is now lost. The majority of connoisseurs consider the Havemeyer version to be the original one and date it between 1810 and 1819.

In 1792 Goya suffered a grave illness which lasted at least two years and left him deaf. He became isolated from the world, lost his previous optimism, and gave a new depth to his art. He worked with astonishing activity until 1828, the year of his death, maintaining his artistic strength and energy. His crusade against the evils of the time, through his engravings, reveals his character as that of a rebel. This was concealed in the day of his early successes, but later manifested itself with great clarity and even cruelty. When to his personal misfortune, and the difficulties created for him by enmity of the Inquisition, was added the catastrophe of the French invasion, Goya saw life in terms of tragedy. His knowledge of Rembrandt's art helped him, and he transformed the colored delicacies of his XVIII century style into violent contrasts of light and shade. Natural appearances were subordinated to constant phantasms of evil. Under the spell of passion, sorrow and indignation, the form became broken, full of accents, open to the mysteries of the unseen world. Goya thus became the first romantic painter.

Majas on a Balcony is an excellent example of the later style of Goya. Two courtesans are seated on a balcony to lure the attention of the passer-by. The light is concentrated on them, on their flesh, on their veils and dresses. Some touches of black in their costumes emphasize the light tones. The purpose of their display is conveyed by the two dark men at the rear. They hide in the half shadow, they look without being seen, they are wrapped in large mantles, they wear menacing hats, their appearance is one of concentrated wickedness. The height of the wall emphasizes the menace. The whole suggests temptation, a plot and a snare. But it is not a genre scene of vicious life. The contrast between the light women and the dark men, between the attractive forms of the courtesans and the repulsive ones of their partners, is dramatic. Not only that, but a certain grandeur in the wickedness of the men suggests the presence of the devil himself.

This magnification of the representation of vice, this flight of fancy beyond the misery of the world, this transcending of the representation of reality, are typical of Goya's poetry. The strength of his imagination carried him always beyond what was possible, towards the absurd, where the comic and the sublime found their unity.

72 · JOHN CONSTABLE

East Bergholt, born 1776, died 1837

Weymouth Bay

Canvas. Height 21 in.; width 30 in.

MUSEUM OF FINE ARTS, BOSTON

Constable's Weymouth Bay came to the Museum of Fine Arts, Boston, from the collection of Mr. and Mrs. William C. Loring in 1930. Its date can be guessed by comparison with other paintings representing the same place: one in the Victoria and Albert Museum, dated 1819, mezzotinted by David Lucas, one in the National Gallery, London, and still another in the Louvre, traditionally considered to have been painted in 1827.

In spite of some differences all three of these paintings show the same style, and must have the same date, which is probably 1819. The style of all is earlier than 1827 and puts in question the traditional date accepted by the Louvre authorities. They represent the bay, but the center of attention seems to be the hill above. In the Boston picture, on the contrary, attention is fixed on the bay itself and its spaciousness. The style is the same, thus the painting must be contemporary with those in London and Paris. Through a pencil drawing we know that Constable painted near Weymouth in November 1816. This date seems too early, as we shall see. The date of 1819 is appropriate also to the Boston picture.

In 1819 Constable was at the beginning of his best period, which lasted until 1825. Before that time his realistic trend prevails, afterwards his romantic tendency predominates. In his happiest years a balance between the different impulses of his imagination is perfectly realized.

His realism was intended to be in opposition to the fashion of neo-classicism, then triumphing, and above all to eclecticism, the combination of the various qualities in painting drawn from the study of the works of the most excellent masters. Constable wanted to forget the experience of the past, and dedicate himself to the "first source" of art, that is, to nature. Through his influence on French painting he founded the realism of the whole XIX century.

Constable was a good painter of portraits, the kind of painting which had the greatest success in England at the beginning of the XIX century. He preferred to paint landscape because he loved the English countryside and because he felt that he could be absolutely original in landscape painting and there discover a new world for art.

It is true that in the XVII and XVIII centuries landscape painting had a rich tradition, but it sprang from a spirit of curiosity and from the picturesque rather than from the love and adoration of nature.

It is the moral approach of Constable which distinguishes his work from everything that was done before. It is his humility before what has been created by God, his conviction that nothing is ugly in nature if it is touched by light, and his ability to reveal his intimate feelings through spots of color, which constitute his originality and his glory. Before a painting of his one feels what he felt when he wrote the year he painted Weymouth Bay: "At every step I take, and on whatever object I turn my eyes, that sublime expression of the Scriptures, 'I am the resurrection and the life,' seems as if uttered near me."

Such is the romantic touch of his painting, such the faith he impressed on the depiction of what he saw.

73 · JOSEPH MALLORD WILLIAM TURNER

London, born 1775, died 1851

St. Mark's Place, or Juliet and Her Nurse

Canvas. Height 35 in.; width 47½ in.

MRS. G. MACCULLOCH MILLER, OLD WESTBURY, L. I.

The first exhibition of this painting was at the Royal Academy in 1836. It then came into the possession of Munro of Novar, a friend of Turner. Subsequently it belonged to the Hodgson collection, London, and the Payne collection, New York. St. Mark's Place is filled by crowds of masquerading figures. Fireworks produce conflicting lights. At the extreme right, on a parapet roof, is Juliet with her nurse. Ruskin thought that the light effect is that of "an hour after sunset, with light of rockets and fire." Sir Walter Armstrong believed that the scene was imagined at "early dawn." The traditional title of the painting is "St. Mark's Place by Moonlight." All this is arbitrary, the moon does not appear in the painting, and the light is an imaginary one, an artificial light due to the fireworks.

When the painting was exhibited at the Royal Academy *Blackwood's Magazine* attacked it violently. Ten days before being matriculated at Oxford, Ruskin, then seventeen years old, answered at length, championing Turner. The reply was not published because Turner did not wish it to be. It became the germ of Ruskin's *Modern Painters*.

What appealed to Ruskin was both the mystery of Turner's imagination and the subtle observation of reality. He saw in Turner the connoisseur of natural history and the fantastic poet. He wrote: "His imagination is Shakespearean in its mightiness. Had the scene of 'Juliet and her Nurse' risen up before the mind of a poet, and been described in 'words that burn,' it had been the admiration of the world. . . . Many-colored mists are floating above the distant city, but such mists as you might imagine to be aetherial spirits, souls of the mighty dead breathed out of the tombs of Italy into the blue of her bright heaven, and wandering in vague and infinite glory around the earth that they have loved. Instinct with the beauty of uncertain light, they move and mingle among the pale stars, and rise up into the brightness of the illimitable heaven, whose soft, sad blue eye gazes down into the deep water of the sea for ever—that sea whose motionless and silent transparency is beaming with phosphor light, that emanates out of its sapphire serenity like bright dreams breathed into the spirit of a deep sleep. And the spires of the glorious city rise indistinctly bright into those living mists, like pyramids of pale fire from some vast altar; and amidst the glory of the dream, there is as it were the voice of a multitude entering by the eye—arising from the stillness of the city like the summer wind passing over the leaves of the forest, when a murmur is heard amidst their multitude. . . . That this picture is not seen by either starlight, sunlight, moonlight, or firelight, is perfectly true: it is a light of his own, which no other artist can produce—a light which seems owing to some phosphorescent property in the air. The picture can be, and ought only to be viewed as embodied enchantment, delineated magic."

It is the glory of this painting to have raised such enthusiasm in the young Ruskin. Since that time Turner has become a kind of national hero of England. He still occupies that position despite the reservation of Roger Fry and other recent critics. They see in Turner the maker of pictures which suggest "vague aspirations and yearnings and half-understood desires" rather than the seer who communicates his feeling about the world to mankind.

Perhaps the critical problem is still open, but it does not diminish the importance of this picture as an outstanding example of Turner's later and most imaginative style.

74 · JACQUES-LOUIS DAVID

Paris, born 1748, died 1825

PORTRAIT OF MADAME HAMELIN

Canvas. Height 49¼ in.; width 37½ in.

This painting came to the Chester Dale Collection from that of H. O. Havemeyer. It was called "Portrait of a Young Girl in White" until the sitter was identified with Madame Hamelin, a Creole born in Santo Domingo, and wife of a Parisian banker. In the fashionable society of the Directoire she was nicknamed "La Jolie Laide," and Chateaubriand, who liked her, said that she possessed two of the characteristics of the French: nobility and frivolity.

The date of the painting must be 1802, because the style of hairdressing is typical of that year. A very similar portrait by David, probably from the same year, is that of his daughter at work on a tapestry (collection of the Marquis de Ludre).

The portrait of Madame Hamelin shows the style of David at a moment very close to that of his most famous portrait, the Madame Recamier of the Louvre, which is two years earlier. His drawing becomes more and more precise, his form is perfectly dense, his plastic quality is emphasized by a background of a single color. Hence the relief of the figure, light on dark, is pure of any realistic detail. Even the chair, the table and the cloth serve to frame the light figure. The features of the young lady are expressed in a classic form, which gives her dignity, and to a certain extent excludes that "charming ugliness" which her malicious friends said she had. However, the classic style does give sufficient recognition of her individual features to maintain her individuality. Eighteenth century tradition has almost disappeared from this painting, in homage to the classic design. The serpentine lines of the pose, however, is an echo of that tradition, and adds a graceful touch to classic form.

The image is conceived as white on black, but the background is not black. The white dress has some colored shadows and transparencies, and the flesh tints warm the white. In other words, color accompanies plastic form in a subdued way, without disturbing it. Finally what gives to the image a breath, which is both vital and artistic, is the ampleness of the surface against which the image is relieved.

David's style has two diverging trends, towards classical abstraction of form, and towards the power of rendering reality. When he was able to unite both trends he achieved his masterpieces, something that happened in many of his portraits. The individual features of the sitter obliged him to stick to reality, while his abstract form had to be modified. The rhetorical content of his historical scenes was excluded, and simple life, with its contingencies, had to be represented. Thus he made a successful effort to find a coincidence between his diverging trends, and his classical form brought to life a certainty, a severity, a feeling for unity, which was the demand of an ideal, the condition of art.

75 · JEAN AUGUSTE DOMINIQUE INGRES

Montauban, born 1780, died 1867

PORTRAIT OF COMTESSE D'HAUSSONVILLE

Canvas. Height 49¾ in.; width 35⅝ in.

Signed by Ingres and dated 1845, this portrait remained in the d'Haussonville family in Paris until it was purchased for the Frick collection in 1927. In a letter to M. Marcotte, June 28, 1845, Ingres has this to say about it: "I have finished this disastrous portrait, which, tired of tormenting me, gave me the most complete success when I exhibited it in my home for four days. Relatives, friends, and above all the father of the sitter, the Duc de Broglie, were enchanted by it, without any objection. Finally to crown the deed, Mr. Thiers while I was absent came to see the portrait accompanied by the sitter herself and told her repeatedly this vulgar joke: 'Ingres must be in love with you to have painted you so.' But all this does not make me proud, and I do not think I have rendered all the graces of that charming model."

Ingres began the study for this portrait in 1842, the date of a sketch in oil belonging to the Comte d'Haussonville, which shows the figure of the sitter in a reversed pose. In the same year Ingres represented the Comtesse with great care and skill, in a very simple dress and in the same pose as in the final picture, in a drawing belonging to the Bonnat Museum at Bayonne. In 1843 Ingres began a new sketch which he finished two years later. Two drawings of 1845 are preserved in the Ingres Museum, Montauban, where one sees his effort to assemble some objects around the figure. From the drawing of 1842 to the final picture, the process is clear. Ingres wanted to enrich not only the dress but the surroundings of the Comtesse, he wanted to create a *furnished portrait*. Hence all the difficulties of which he complained.

Having put a mirror on the wall where the image of the Comtesse would be reflected, he needed an effect of color, a nuance of light and shade. But color was banned by his theory and reduced to a simple tint. He repeatedly emphasized this, as when he wrote: "Drawing contains everything except the tint." "The line is the drawing, is everything." "If I should put a sign over my door, I should write: *School of Drawing*, and I am sure that I should make painters." "Narrow reflections into shadow, reflections along the contours, are unworthy of the majesty of art."

A reflection in a mirror, the play of folds of a rich, silk dress, could not be rendered by line and drawing alone. Thus Ingres was compelled to go beyond his theory. He was obliged to approach, by choosing a subtle variety of local tones, the chromatic luxury of the contemporaries he furiously detested. A comparison with the "Portrait of Madame Hamelin" (No. 74) shows that David refrained from an effect of coloring, while Ingres found it necessary to use color as a means of connecting his figure with her surroundings. He succeeded, after a great effort. The face and arms of the Comtesse are characteristic of Ingres, all the rest is quite exceptional for him.

His image is a beautiful young woman, an aristocratic one of the Louis Philippe period, of a distinction a little too material, based on wealth. Thus he approaches the representation of an individual life at a given moment, with a given culture. In spite of his classical faith, Ingres reveals here his romantic longing, and creates one of his greatest masterpieces.

76 · FERDINAND VICTOR EUGÈNE DELACROIX

Charenton—Saint-Maurice, born 1798, died 1863

DEATH OF SARDANAPALUS

Canvas. Height 29⅛ in.; width 36⅝ in.

HENRY P. MC ILHENNY, PHILADELPHIA

This is a replica made by Delacroix in 1844 of his composition painted in 1827, now in the Louvre. This replica was bequeathed by Delacroix to the executor of his will, Legrand. It was in the Crabbe and Bellino collections before it came to Mr. McIlhenny.

The subject was inspired by the drama of Byron. It represents Sardanapalus, the King of Niniveh, while he waits for death by fire in his palace, after having ordered that his women and his treasures be burnt with him.

Delacroix wanted to contrast his Oriental subject with the Greek scenes of the painter David, his burning colors with neo-classic form, his moving crowds with the statuary figures of the school of David. He painted the scene of 1827 in six months as a manifesto of the romantics against the neo-classicists. When exhibited at the Salon, his Sardanapalus was a failure. Even those who sympathized with the dawn of romanticism thought that Delacroix made a mistake by exaggerating the scene of horror and the confusion of the composition. They thought that the painting put the whole of romanticism in danger. Victor Hugo alone supported the painter. The Government, which had previously been favorable to him, was alarmed by the general reaction against him, and withdrew all further commissions. These were resumed only after the revolution of 1830.

Many drawings show how carefully Delacroix had prepared his composition. Some of them are studies of Persian miniatures, which suggested to him certain gestures and poses. His warm color was inspired by Bonington.

All this gives the picture of 1827 great importance for a revolution in taste which a whole generation of painters had at heart. In spite of certain marvelous details, however, even today it raises some doubts. An explanation of the relative failure of that painting as a work of art has been offered: Delacroix, under his deep impression from Byron, conceived a scene of blood and horror, and painted a powerful sketch (also in the Louvre) where the figures were few and the general effect of light and shade was well conceived. But when he executed his large picture he was seduced by the beautiful flesh of a model and stressed the effect of sensuality, losing sight of the ensemble. That is, he finished the single figures too highly and disorganized his composition.

As a matter of fact, some of his early compositions were indeed too polemical to be perfect works of art. When, in later years, he returned to them and repeated them for himself at a smaller size, he avoided virtuosity of execution. He did not finish too highly and he created some of his finest paintings. This is the case with this replica of 1844. The central diagonal zone assumes, more successfully than in 1827, its function of light between the two dark corners below at the left and above at the right. Even the palace in the background accompanies the whole scene by its transverse direction, which is not so in the Louvre picture. There some beautiful nude figures stand alone, while in the replica every figure obeys the order of the whole composition. The rhythm of light and dark has no interruption; it has its own value. The execution is fluent, nothing distracts the painter from his pictorial aim.

In 1827 Delacroix was too close to his subject, to his competition with reality, to virtuosity of execution, and to his desire to be striking. In 1844 he was detached enough from all this, and could look at the whole with that disinterestedness which is a requisite condition of art.

77 · JEAN BAPTISTE CAMILLE COROT

Paris, born 1796, died 1875

AGOSTINA

Canvas. Height 51¼ in.; width 37½ in.

Agostina was an Italian model who sat in Corot's studio in Paris during February, 1866, as we know from a sketch of her by his pupil Lavieille which bears an inscription stating it was made in Corot's studio during that month.

When the painting was exhibited at the École des Beaux-Arts, Paris, in 1875, at the first retrospective exhibition of Corot, it belonged to M. Breysse. It then went through the collections of Faure, Paton and Bernheim-Jeune and finally to that of Chester Dale in New York.

In his painting of figures Corot achieved some of his masterpieces. His contemporaries, however, did not appreciate these, and Corot exhibited them at the Salon only twice, in 1840 and in 1869. He said that the aim of his life was to paint landscapes. In 1874 he refused to exhibit a figure because he did not want to compete with it for a prize which the jury continued to refuse to his landscapes. It is only within the last thirty years that the critics as well as the public have come to realize the absolute value of Corot's figures, and sometimes have even preferred them to his landscapes.

The main reason for the former indifference and the present enthusiasm for the figures of Corot is that they are not conceived in the traditional academic way. The process of Ingres, for example, in painting a figure was to begin by drawing its formal interior construction, and to arrive at its appearance on the surface only at the moment of the final finish. Corot on the contrary bathed his figures in the light and the atmosphere of his landscapes. It was only by the last touch that he achieved a solid form. The process from inside to outside is typical of the classicistic tradition, while the other process from outside to inside is typical of the Impressionists. Corot foreshadowed the impressionistic trend, and this is one of the reasons for the present enthusiasm for him.

Agostina was a woman with classic features: strong, severe, without graciousness but with noble proportions. She had imposing character and the plastic quality which are connected with the idea of beauty. Corot was attracted by her sculptural appearance, by her full figure and her rounded shoulders, which recalled to him his youthful years in Rome. But his style was not sculptural at all, and his feeling was not thoroughly sympathetic with his model. Thus while bowing to her objective beauty, he transformed her in a vision of his own. The blue of the sleeves, the fanciful ornaments of the gown, the relation between the brown of the gown and that of the landscape transform the sculptural model into the picturesque style of Corot. The large shadow on the cheek also lessens the plastic value of the face. This contrast between the character of the model and the feeling and the visualizing of the painter could become an obstacle to the artistic perfection of the painting. But Corot, with his usual ease, overcomes any difficulty and succeeds in creating one of his strongest and most imposing figures.

78 · HONORÉ DAUMIER

Marseilles, born 1808, died 1879

THIRD CLASS RAILWAY CARRIAGE

Canvas. Height 25¾ in.; width 35½ in.

HAVEMEYER COLLECTION. METROPOLITAN MUSEUM OF ART, NEW YORK

This painting entered the Havemeyer collection after being in the Duz collection and that of C. D. Borden of Boston. The subject was treated by Daumier more than once. The earliest version is a water-color of the same composition in the Walters Art Gallery, Baltimore. Another watercolor of a third class carriage, with an entirely different composition, was in the Gerstenberg Collection, Berlin.

Daumier devoted himself to painting chiefly in the last decades of his life, when he became more and more detached from the lithographs which gave him renown. The date of this painting has been considered to be between 1860 and 1870.

Henri Marceau and David Rosen have demonstrated by infra-red photographs that Daumier painted the Metropolitan example by enlarging the Walters watercolor. He employed the method of squaring and emphasized strong lines constructing forms. Only then did he begin to cover the outlines with layers of colored pigment. This process, which was necessary to complete the painting, was interrupted.

Theoretically every time a painter considers that he has expressed what he has to say, his painting is finished, even though his images have no objective illusionary appearance. Compared with a painting of Ingres, for instance, the painting is not finished, and it does not reach that limit of finish that is usual in Daumier. The Metropolitan picture, however, has its own quality which depends above all on the stress on individual characters, on their vital energy, on their potential movement. As far as this quality is concerned, this painting can be considered finished and perfect, as is true of most sketches.

Here one must emphasize the value of Daumier as a painter, not merely as a draughtsman. We need only look at the infra-red photograph of the Third Class Carriage to understand that the drawing, wonderful as it is, by no means exhausts the quality of the painting. The brown shadow which envelops every image, and in which are some subdued blue, red and rose tones, gives a visionary aspect to every object.

Daumier is a realist in the sense that he does not participate in romantic fancy or in the romantic fallacy. He sticks to the life around him and wants to represent the character of what he sees. His lithographs embody a constant struggle against those who oppress mankind by political and social power, or by wealth. But when he represents people traveling in a third class carriage, he is not hostile to anyone and paints his characters in order to reveal their human, simple life and nothing else. It was difficult at the time of Daumier to interest art lovers in the simple life of the man of the street. Thus Daumier painted for himself. His subject matter is that of everyday life, and is thus thoroughly realistic.

His realism, however, was of a special kind. He did not care to paint directly from the model, he always painted from memory. His visual memory was extremely keen, and he could always portray a gesture which revealed a whole character. The simplifications which memory requires were necessary to emphasize a character, a meaning, or an action. His realism became, therefore, the forerunner of symbolism and expressionism. Hence the tremendous influence Daumier has had on later painting. Beyond all this one can see in his work a certainty, a ripeness and a monumentality which form the intimate value of his art.

170

79 · GUSTAVE COURBET

Ornans, born 1819, died 1877

LADY IN A RIDING HABIT

Canvas. Height 45½ in.; width 35⅛ in.

HAVEMEYER COLLECTION. METROPOLITAN MUSEUM OF ART, NEW YORK

Zacharie Astruc, an intelligent French critic, published in 1859 a plea for the art of Courbet against the misunderstandings of the French public. He had visited Courbet's studio and seen his Lady in a Riding Habit which he described accurately and praised highly. "What a delicious canvas! The lady is above all charming, very noble, elegant; her beautiful black eyes have a pure radiation, so chaste, so reserved, that one is moved; her cheeks are of a miraculous freshness. The blood pulses there very strongly. As for the painting it is difficult to explain its charm and truth. The white and rose tones of the face, the depth and the limpidity of the eyes, the fine harmony of tones so well fused, the perfect nobility of the pose: this is a portrait which will have a great renown later, when the painter shall send it to one of our future exhibitions. No impudent critic will dare to say that Courbet lacks the intimate sense of elegance. Elegance exists in nature, and Courbet sees it better than anyone else." It does not seem that Courbet ever did exhibit this portrait.

The sitter is Louise Colet, born in 1810, author of poems, novels and memoirs, famous for her salon in Paris and her relations with Victor Cousin, Alphonse Karr and above all Gustave Flaubert. In 1856 she was in love with Champfleury, who did not respond to her advances and introduced to her his friend Courbet. He thus painted her portrait about that year. In 1856 Courbet had created almost all his masterpieces: The Stonebreakers is of 1848, The Burial at Ornans of 1849, the Atelier of 1855. In this latter year he had held his one-man exhibition, which was an artistic scandal and gave him a wide-spread renown. His visualization was fully mature, his creative power was at its acme, his confidence in himself was absolute, and he was perfectly free from the compromises with academic drawing which began a little later.

Courbet was the founder and the most outspoken representative of *realism* in art. Of course his realism was of a special kind, at once a consequence of romanticism and a reaction against romanticism. Romantics believed in an ideal, which they drew from poetry, and allowed themselves some daring flights of imagination. On the contrary Courbet wanted to stay close to nature and to paint only what he saw. But his sure drawing and his subdued harmony of colors did not belong to nature: they belonged to the romantic tradition. Furthermore the dreamy expression he thought to find in nature was his own ideal, even though he was not clearly conscious of it. What he was conscious of was his power of subordinating nature to his will. "To know in order to be powerful" was his motto. It was the motto of a conqueror.

He knew that he was a handsome man and was very proud of it. One may guess that Louise Colet, then forty-six, after her disappointment with Champfleury, liked Courbet. But Courbet was an uneducated man, with manners and experience quite inferior to those of the literate Louise Colet. He admired her, her distinction, her elegance, her pretention to nobility. All this is very well impressed on the portrait. He did not insist on the full roundness of the form, or on the details of the face. To insist would have meant to approach too close to reality. He restrained himself, framed with black the white face, so that the contrast between light and dark zones would result in a certain delicacy of appearance. Her glance, which appeared chaste to Astruc, is mysterious in order to be tempting. The riding habit gives the suggestion of nobility and elegance. The romantic landscape betrays a lover's contemplation.

In portraying Louise Colet, Courbet dedicated his power as a realist painter to an ideal which aimed at social homage but actually reveals his naïve admiration.

172

82 · ALBERT PINKHAM RYDER

New Bedford, Mass., born 1847, died 1917

MOONLIGHT — MARINE

Wood. Height 11⅜ in.; width 12 in.

METROPOLITAN MUSEUM OF ART, NEW YORK

It is difficult to believe that the painting of Ryder could be contemporary with that of Homer or Eakins. Yet it is true that at a time of such naturalism and objectivity in painting, a fanciful poet could paint as Ryder did. This indicates how many sided was that period of art.

Ryder was essentially a self-taught painter. He had, however, studied under William Marshall, who had been a pupil of Couture. This may explain the thickness of the pigment used by Ryder. When he went to Paris he was interested above all by Corot and Maris. The romanticism of Maris may have suggested something to him. However, there is no doubt that in the history of art it is difficult to find a man so independent and solitary as was Ryder.

He was a romantic, inspired by poets, "soaked in the moonlight." His strength lay in carrying his romanticism to the extreme, without any compromise with academic tradition which lowered the creativity of so many romanticists. To be a romanticist at the end of the XIX century meant to be a survivor of a past age. Ryder longed for the expression of his enthusiasm, of his mysticism, of his enchantment before the mystery of nature. Because he did not care for anything but the intensity of his expression, he simplified the shape of things to the utmost. Thus he reached a kind of abstract art, abstract from the external world, in order to reveal his intimate mood. As a romanticist, he was a survivor, as an abstractionist he was a prophet. It is natural that he is revered today as a great artist and a great forerunner.

By disregarding the representation of things he was brought to wish his paintings to be precious objects in themselves, and his colors to be like enamels. Thus he superimposed layer after layer of color, and worked at a painting for years upon years. When he succeeded his hues are radiant, when he did not his pictures went physically to pieces. This effort to master the technique of the impossible was the torment of his life. He once said: "Have you ever seen an inchworm crawl up a leaf or twig, and there, clinging to the very end, revolve in the air, feeling for something, to reach something? That's like me. I am trying to find something out there beyond the place on which I have a footing." Supported by such humor and such modesty Ryder was able to face the mystery of the universe.

Again and again he painted the moonlight on the sea. His preference can be well understood. Nothing is simpler than a sea and a sky, and a dark sailboat. His form was as simple as the motif, and the contrast of light and shade, not tied with reality, was the very expression of his dreaming contemplation. Our Moonlight—Marine is a perfect example of his abstract form and of his concrete imagination.

83 · EDOUARD MANET

Paris, born 1832, died 1883

IN A BOAT

Canvas. Height 38¼ in.; width 51¼ in.

HAVEMEYER COLLECTION. METROPOLITAN MUSEUM OF ART, NEW YORK

This signed painting was executed in 1874 and exhibited at the Salon of 1879, where M. Desfossés bought it. Later it was sold to Mrs. Havemeyer. The figures portrayed are Madame Manet and her brother Rodolphe Leenhoff.

In August 1874 Manet went to Argenteuil to be with Claude Monet and his family. There he worked up paintings he had left unfinished and completed two of them: Argenteuil (Tournai Museum) and In a Boat. The latter was the most daring, as it completely renounced plastic values. Perhaps for this reason Manet exhibited at the Salon of 1875 only the Argenteuil and did not venture to exhibit In a Boat until four years later. The Argenteuil, however, had a very unfavorable reception, while In a Boat in 1879 was praised by Huysmans and even by De Swarte, in spite of his opinion that it was unfinished.

The fact is that, either as a result of the presence of Monet or of the season, so inviting to painting out of doors, that summer at Argenteuil was a turning point in the style of Manet. If one compares In a Boat with The Railroad (Le Chemin de Fer, Havemeyer Collection) which is of 1873, one sees the same pictorial motif, that is, figures detached from the background instead of relieved against the background. This had been a preference of Manet ever since the 'sixties, to renounce the traditional plastic values in favor of the effect of contrasting colors. But in 1873 the form was still too fixed, with contour lines too marked, to give the impression of images created by color. On the contrary in 1874 such an impression is self-evident. Argenteuil shows forms created by color with some sharp contrasts of light and shade and a space shown approximately in perspective. In a Boat renounces even the horizon; blue water is the only background of the figures. These of course are not flat, because the sunlight forms their volumes, which have the characteristic appearance of an atmospheric mass, where the light enters much more freely than into solid matter. Hence the images acquire lightness, ease, the poetry which is proper to the phantasm, to the unreal, to legend.

Claude Monet called a boat, where he liked to paint, his "studio." Manet twice portrayed his friend and Madame Monet in the boat, but left the two sketches unfinished. No doubt they were the first idea for In a Boat. This was finished to perfection: any further precision would have destroyed the effect of light and color.

It is well known that during the 'sixties Manet modified the traditional conception of form, thus opening the way to the Impressionists. But the new trend which was called Impressionism was realized around 1870 by Monet, Renoir and Pissarro, by clarifying the palette and by using division of colors. Manet gradually approached the new trend, through a sketchy and nervous form, and with In a Boat, perhaps for the first time, he attained a fully impressionistic vision, which later he almost constantly pursued.

His personality of course did not change, and we recognize it in the abruptness of the semblance, in the completeness of realization, against the accepted principles, in the distinction he always impresses in his images. But In a Boat suggests to us something else, a new boldness, a new detachment from reality, in short a joy in the discovery of a new vision and a new ideal. We feel in this the presence of a masterpiece.

84 · EDGAR HILAIRE GERMAIN DEGAS

Paris, born 1834, died 1917

REHEARSAL OF THE BALLET ON THE STAGE

Paper mounted on canvas. Height 21⅜ in.; width 28¾ in.

HAVEMEYER COLLECTION. METROPOLITAN MUSEUM OF ART, NEW YORK

Exhibited at the Centennial Exposition in Paris, 1900, when owned by Mrs. Cobden Sickert, this signed painting was later bought by Mrs. Havemeyer.

The stage is seen from the side; in the background are seated two of the directors of the theatre, in the middle distance the rehearsal proceeds under the orders of the ballet master, while in the foreground are dancers resting, waiting for their turn. This motif was repeated by Degas three times in 1874. What is probably the first one, painted in grisaille, is in the Louvre. There Degas was interested by the representation of the perspective space of the stage: thus he emphasized the rounded external limit of the scene and the dark background, in order to stress the plastic forms of the dancers, with fixed contours and graduations of chiaroscuro. He sought also to show the space in depth, dividing the dancers rehearsing from those resting, and eliminating the figure of the ballet master.

On the contrary in the Havemeyer painting, which is multicolored and not monochrome, he did not seek representation of space in depth. Thus he abolished the external limit of the stage, showed the floor rising towards the surface, put the ballet master intermediately between the two groups of dancers and extended to the middle of the stage the picturesque foliage of the side scenes. By so doing he effected a complete change of vision. In the Paris painting he shows a space filled with plastic figures, in the Havemeyer painting he shows a picturesque background from which certain light and certain dark tones emerge in a thick atmosphere.

Degas repeated the same motif a third time in a pastel (also in the Havemeyer Collection at the Metropolitan, from the May Collection) which shows little variation from the previous one.

The change of vision from the Paris example to the two Havemeyer pictures can be explained by the very date of 1874. It was the year of the first exhibition of the Impressionists, in which Degas participated. His beginnings, it is true, had been very different from those of the other Impressionists. Degas was a master of academic drawing, the greatest master since Ingres, and he was proud of it. He despised the ideal of pantheism, the love of nature, the sacrifice of plastic form to effects of light through colors, which constituted the basis of the impressionistic taste. But he was intelligent enough to understand that academic drawing was dead in art, and that to create a living form he should assimilate some of the pictorial qualities of the Impressionists. The renouncement of the space in depth, the rhythm of light and dark tones, the variety of colors, the extension of the picturesque by the side scenes: all this was the tribute he paid to impressionistic taste. But he retained something of his previous preferences: the well rounded arms and legs of the dancers show a purity and a certainty of drawing which are typical of Degas.

His companions admired Degas for his power of drawing, and the critics and the public who did not accept impressionistic principles were only too glad to find a painter who fully satisfied at least one of the so-called laws of art. Today also his irreproachable drawing is the main reason of the fame of Degas.

From a critical point of view what counts is not that perfect drawing in itself, but the finesse and sensibility which allowed Degas to find a relation between his drawing and pictorial effect, where the drawing is a touch of distinction, subtlety, of ideal beauty, a suggestion of imaginary forms even to the point of deformation. The Havemeyer Rehearsal of the Ballet on the Stage is a perfect example of this artistic value.

85 · CLAUDE MONET

Paris, born 1840, died 1926

BANKS OF THE SEINE, VÉTHEUIL

Canvas. Height 29 in.; width 39½ in.

CHESTER DALE COLLECTION. NATIONAL GALLERY OF ART, WASHINGTON

The painting, signed and dated 1880, has been in the United States since 1890 or 1892, when it was exhibited at the American Art Association. From the collection of James F. Sutton, New York, it entered the Chester Dale Collection.

Monet lived at Vétheuil from 1878 to 1881, when, after many years close to starvation, he felt that success was approaching. At the fourth exhibition of the Impressionists in 1879 Monet exhibited twenty-nine canvases; at the fifth exhibition in 1880, none. He detached himself from his comrades, and occasioned the crisis of the Impressionist group. The reason he gave for his withdrawal was that the group opened its doors "to any new-come dauber" (perhaps an allusion to Gauguin), but the true reason seems to have been his desire to fight alone, in order to achieve success more rapidly. A one-man show in 1880 was indeed good advertising for Monet.

Monet is considered the leader of Impressionism, and indeed he contributed a great deal to it. It was he who decided to finish his pictures out of doors, in order to be faithful to the effect of light. Furthermore he divided colors with greater decision than his companions. A green can be obtained by the mixture of blue and yellow. If you mix the two tints, you obtain a green, but not an intense one, rather a grey-green. If on the contrary you put on the canvas two touches of pure blue and pure yellow, one close to the other, the spectator from a certain distance sees the green as much more intense than if it had been the result of a mixture of tints. By dividing colors, the Impressionists obtained a perceptible or optical mixture of colors rather than a material mixture of pigments. Monet and Renoir drew inspiration for their division of colors from the reflections of light on the water, the observation of a phenomenon of nature became a principle of style in painting.

Impressionism was a very complex movement. What Monet contributed was above all the principle of "plein-airism" and the division of colors. For some years his style was very close to that of the other Impressionists. In 1877, however, he began his series of the railroad station of Saint-Lazare in Paris, which, together with his Vétheuil paintings, show the beginning of a new trend, fully personal. His detachment from his companions was the result of disagreement not only in practical matters, but also in artistic trend.

Ever since the beginning of Impressionism some critics have understood that Monet was much less a realist than, for an example, Pissarro. He sought inspiration from exceptional effects rather than from the every day life of nature, in order to develop his own fancy. This desire for the exceptional, the surprising effect, augmented from 1877 onwards. The late springtime suggested to Monet his Banks of the Seine, Vétheuil, where the touches of light in the water and in the flowers create a fanciful excitement. In that same year 1880 Théodore Duret, the critic, considered Monet the most inventive and the most original among the landscapists of his time. Perhaps he was right; and this is what justified belief in the leadership of Monet—not that he was the best painter. In anxious research for an effect he lost sometimes that detachment of the mind from workmanship which perfect art requires. He was a fighter; we surprise him in the midst of his battle; he won and we admire him. But we also feel that in the happy fight something was lost. In a painting like this one, we are not aware of the dangers inherent in Monet's luminism, but in later works his ability to realize his fancy became more and more arbitrary. No one can deny that in his Vétheuil paintings his greatness is still living.

86 · CAMILLE PISSARRO

Saint-Thomas-des-Antilles, born 1830, died 1903

BOULEVARD DES ITALIENS, MORNING, SUNLIGHT

Canvas. Height 38¾ in.; width 36¼ in.

CHESTER DALE COLLECTION. NATIONAL GALLERY OF ART, WASHINGTON

Before entering the Chester Dale Collection, this painting, signed and dated 1897, was in the Lessing collection, Berlin. In a letter from Eragny of February 8, 1897, Camille Pissarro wrote to his son Lucien: "I am returning to Paris again on the tenth, to do a series of the boulevard des Italiens . . . I engaged a large room at the Grand Hôtel de Russie, 1 rue Drouot, from which I can see the whole sweep of boulevards almost as far as the Porte Saint-Denis, anyway as far as the boulevard Bonne Nouvelle." From the rue Drouot he could see at the right the Boulevard des Italiens and at the left the Boulevard Montmartre.

As the painting here illustrated looks towards the right, it represents the Boulevard des Italiens, not the Boulevard Montmartre as it has sometimes been called. We know thirteen canvases painted by Pissarro in 1897 of the Boulevard Montmartre and only two of the Boulevard des Italiens: the one here illustrated and another in the Lewisohn collection, New York. All were finished in April 1897, and exhibited at the Durand-Ruel Gallery in Paris in 1898.

Pissarro had painted in previous years views of streets and buildings in Paris and in Rouen, but the pictures of the boulevards of 1897 began a new type in his work, which had success, and which he repeated in his last years. To paint a street from an upper window meant to upset the usual perspective vision, and transform the pavement into a background for the crowd, the buses and the trees. Thus the surface of the painting reacquires its rights, and it is on the surface that appear the multicolored sketchy images, vibrating as touches of light and shade, in a continuous movement. Such an impressionistic vision of a boulevard was new, it lacked the objective representation of a reality dear to the public at large, but acquired a power of life unknown in the views of towns painted before.

Pissarro had been, towards 1870, one of the founders of Impressionism, and contributed to it his structural sense, which was stronger than that of Monet, Sisley or Renoir. Besides, Pissarro was older than the other Impressionists, and, being very generous and of the conviction of a prophet, he suggested his structural principles to Monet, and taught his impressionistic vision to Cézanne, Gauguin and Seurat. But he was also enthusiastic about the novelties of other painters, thus he was influenced by Monet, Cézanne and Seurat, transforming himself into a pupil after having been a teacher. For some years in the 'eighties he followed Seurat, his "pointillism" and his geometric constructions. But later he understood that his own temperament could not afford the discipline of pointillism without losing the free expression of his sensibility, and he tried to go back to his impressionistic style of the 'seventies. He could not, because his interest could not be limited any longer to meadows and trees. He needed a new motif and he found it in the crowds and variety of the boulevards in Paris. His motif and his way of painting coincided, and he achieved several masterpieces. Among them Boulevard des Italiens, Morning, Sunlight is of the first rank. From 1896 to 1903, the year of his death, Pissarro had indeed a revival of his creative power, an expression of his poetic feeling through enthusiasm for light, movement, modern life and love for mankind, with a moral as well as an aesthetic accent.

87 · PIERRE AUGUSTE RENOIR

Limoges, born 1841, died 1919

MOTHER AND CHILDREN

Canvas. Height 66⅛ in.; width 41⅜ in.

FRICK COLLECTION, NEW YORK

Renoir's Mother and Children was painted about 1874, the very year the Impressionists exhibited together for the first time. It reveals the early impressionistic style of Renoir. In landscape painting he had already created his own impressionistic form in 1869. In figure-painting, however, he remained under the influence of the darker palettes of Courbet and Manet until 1874. At that time Renoir was living in Paris and often visited Monet at nearby Argenteuil. Renoir's Mother and Children has a style very close to his Madame Monet Reading the *Figaro* (National Gallery, London) and Madame Monet and Her Son in Their Garden (Michel Monet Collection, Giverny), painted in or about 1874, with their new light and brilliance, already familiar in Impressionist landscape.

Renoir was the companion of Monet painting on the river Seine, and both began to extend to all images the division of colors observed in the reflections on water. He was thus one of the early founders of Impressionism.

Monet, Pissarro or Sisley painted chiefly landscapes, where this principle of style could be easily applied.

Renoir, however, was too fond of women's beauty and children's grace, of the easy going life of Paris, for him to remain in the country the whole year to study the changing lights in the fields and the trees, in the hills and the sky. Thus he faced the problem of interpreting human forms through the impressionistic principle of style.

He could not emphasize the structure of his images, without losing the vibrations of light, nor could he stress space in depth, without accentuating a composition of lines. Thus he laid his emphasis on the surface, where his images are luminous visions, immersed in a vibrating atmosphere, and are created by colors and lights rather than by plastic form.

Experienced and subtle colorist that Renoir is, his soul is that of a dreamer of dreams, and his painting has the charm of the primitive. His images exist only in the world of fancy, they are full of grace, they smile not through their lips but through their colors and poses. The touch of humor in them is very subtle. They are fairies, and the whole painting is a work of the fairies.

This dreamlike aspect of the art of Renoir must be emphasized because of the confusion which still persists between realism and Impressionism. Impressionism was actually the first step away from reality, in order to build up an autonomous world of painting. What has been thought realistic in Renoir is his power of impressing life, even on a doll. This is the life of art, not of physical nature—a life free from any rule except that of creation, where the irregularity, the improvised invention, the pure pleasure of painting, find their own rhythm, and thus produce a new kind of beauty.

88 · PIERRE AUGUSTE RENOIR

Limoges, born 1841, died 1919

LUNCHEON OF THE BOATING PARTY

Canvas. Height 51 in.; width 68 in.

PHILLIPS MEMORIAL GALLERY, WASHINGTON

Renoir painted this picture in 1881 at the tavern of the "mère Fournaise" at Bougival, portraying his friends and models. The girl in the foreground playing with a small dog is Alice Charigat, who later became Madame Renoir. Behind her is the son of Fournaise; at the right, still in the foreground, is the painter Caillebotte. The man seen from the back is a bohemian, Baron Barbier. Another model, Angèle, who posed also for the Femme au Chat by Renoir, appears twice in the picture: near Caillebotte and a little further, drinking. A literary man by the name of Maggiolo leans towards her near Caillebotte. The gentleman with a top hat in the background is the art-critic, Renoir's friend, Ephrussi. Two other men represent L'hote, the painter, and Lestringuez. This is a scene of the bohemian life which Renoir enjoyed and which inspired also his Moulin de la Galette, painted in 1876 (Louvre). Some years had passed since then and the Luncheon of the Boating Party shows Renoir's growing preference for variety of colors, suggestion of space and solidity of forms, which did not exist previously in his work.

In 1881, the date of this painting, his years of misery and poverty were past, and he had a limited but faithful group of clients. While trying to please them with portraits, he indulged too much in conventionality, but when he returned to the bohemian life of his friends, he regained his complete freedom and consequent creative power. Here people are indulging in the pleasures of eating and drinking, with a refinement, intelligence, brilliant distinction and subtle gaiety which is the secret of Parisian life. This life was Renoir's ideal. The object of the ideal was mediocre, but the ideal itself was high. A gentle grace emanates from the faces, the clothing, the fruit, the tablecloth, and even the atmosphere itself. That grace is realized in light—a light which is flowering, fleeting, skimming, appearing and disappearing, giving a vibration to everyone, even those seated—a cosmic vibration. It is not a purely physical light. Its vibration is a smile—the smile of youth, of life, of the gayest season of the year, and finally of love.

By the beginning of the year 1881, Renoir was finally making money, and France was not large enough to spend it in. He went to Algiers. From there he planned to go to London, where his friend, Duret, the critic, was living. To this end he even began to study English, but his good resolution lasted only until he reached Paris on the eighteenth of April. There, as he wrote to Duret, he found too many flowers and charming women, and could not leave. He fell in love with Alice Charigat and it was at this time that he painted the picture. It was a happy moment, a turning point in his life as well as in his art.

The boating party pleased Renoir by its easy behavior, which inspired him to a free form. There is no ulterior reason why these people are moving, acting, appearing—no reason but life itself. The figures, the subject matter have no aim, no special significance. The expression has been transferred from the subject matter to the form, which is the form of light and colors.

In a certain sense this painting ends the impressionistic period of Renoir. In the autumn of the same year 1881, he went to Italy, studied Raphael, and tried to follow a new path. Renoir could not have achieved a more glorious conclusion of the years of his youth.

89 · PIERRE AUGUSTE RENOIR

Limoges, born 1841, died 1919

THE DANCE AT BOUGIVAL

Canvas. Height 70 in.; width 38 in.

MUSEUM OF FINE ARTS, BOSTON

This painting, signed and dated 1883, was in the Barret-Decap collection, Biarritz, before it came to the Boston Museum.

Suzanne Valadon, later a painter and the mother of Utrillo, affirmed that she had been the model for the girl in this picture. The man seems to have been Lestringuez. In the same year 1883 Renoir painted two companion pictures The Dance in the Country and The Dance in Town. The Dance at Bougival is perhaps a reelaboration of The Dance in the Country with a bettered design of the group and a clearer realization of the movement. Compared with the Luncheon of the Boating Party, painted only two years earlier, The Dance at Bougival shows clearly a new strength, a new rhythm, a new unity. The impressionistic atmosphere is confined to the background, the two principal figures appear with a new intensity of colors and a new design.

What has happened? In the autumn of 1881 Renoir went to Italy, to Venice, and then to Rome. From Naples he wrote to Durand-Ruel on November 21: "I have been to see the Raphaels in Rome. They are really beautiful and I should have seen them before. They are full of knowledge and wisdom. He did not seek the impossible, as I did." What was the impossible? The reflections of light, and the division of colors. Later he admitted: "Around 1883 a sort of break occurred in my work. I had gone to the end of Impressionism and I was reaching the conclusion that I didn't know either how to paint or how to draw. In a word, I was at a dead end." It was a crisis and fortunately a transient one. In the effort to overcome it, he created The Dance at Bougival, a masterpiece. The balance is perfect between drawing and color, the solidity of forms and the intensity of colors, the occupation of space in depth and the extension on the surface. It is an expression of the easygoing life which Renoir enjoyed, but with a new certainty and authority. In later works his effort to emphasize his lines drew him far from what his creative imagination required, towards a certain academic dryness at the expense of coloring. But this is not the case with The Dance at Bougival.

A good defense against the dangers of academic taste he found in his own theory. He wrote in 1884 a project for an association to advance his ideas. He stated that in art as in nature, all beauty is irregular. Two eyes, when they are beautiful, are never entirely alike. Neither is a nose, when it is finely drawn, exactly above the middle of the mouth. Segments of an orange, the foliage of a tree, the petals of a flower are never identical. Beauty of every description finds its charm in variety. Nature abhors both vacuum and regularity. For the same reason, no work of art can really be called such if it has not been created by an artist who believes in irregularity and rejects any set form. Regularity, order, desire for perfection (which is always a false perfection) destroy art. The only possibility of maintaining taste in art is to impress on artists and the public the importance of irregularity. Irregularity is the basis of all art.

If one remembers how strongly the classic tradition required order and regularity, one understands that Renoir could not become a classicist. In fact after some deviations and some happy efforts, Renoir found again the easy path to creation that was suited to his genius.

Aix-en-Provence, born 1839, died 1906

MOUNT SAINTE-VICTOIRE

Canvas. Height 23⅝ in.; width 28¾ in.

PHILLIPS MEMORIAL GALLERY, WASHINGTON

From the Reber collection, Lausanne, this work passed to the Phillips collection. It may be dated 1885-1887. In these years Cézanne completed and perfected a momentous development in his art. In his youthful years he had worked out a magic realism; then, between 1872 and 1878, he assimilated the impressionistic trend under the influence of Camille Pissarro. The most important effort the Impressionists made together, in order to conquer the favor of the public, was the exhibition of 1877. Cézanne participated in it with sixteen paintings and watercolors. From the practical point of view the exhibition was a failure, and Cézanne retired; he did not exhibit any longer with his friends. From 1883 to 1887 he lived in and near Aix-en-Provence, far from Paris, its exhibitions, its artistic movements. He conceded that the reason of his retirement was the search for a theory which could justify his style.

Impressionism had allowed him to develop his sensibility for color relations, to obtain a form from the contrasts and the nuances of light and shade, to be free in front of nature from all the residues of romanticism which were connected with the magic realism of his early period. His sensibility being extraordinarily keen, Cézanne was aware that it needed a rigorous frame of mind, a structural order. Any order in art is abstraction. Hence the new trend of Cézanne was towards abstraction, but his order was essentially different from everything that had been done before, because he did not impose his order on his sensations but tried to find order in his sensations. In other words, he did not close his colors and lights within a preconceived form, but extracted a new form from his masses of colors, thus letting order and sensation coincide.

Between 1885 and 1887 this process was perfected and he created some of his masterpieces. One of them is the Mount Sainte-Victoire here illustrated.

Cézanne loved this mountain, which dominates the valley around Aix-en-Provence, and portrayed it many times. Here he represented it with a large part of the valley, thus emphasizing its monumentality. Two pine trees in the foreground frame the view in a decorative mood, and accompany the line of the mountain. The main interpretation of the view, however, is constructive and not decorative. Houses, roads, fields and so on are situated each on a determined plane, and all the planes form a structure which has its own artistic value beyond the representations of reality. Thus the mountain appears much more distinct than in reality, but its distance is very well felt. That is to say, the organism of the different planes is autonomous, it belongs to art rather than to nature, it is a new nature, the product of imagination. Hence the majesty of the picture, like that of a sacred shrine, its calm and solidity, proper to things eternal, its essentiality, from which anything contingent is excluded and in which any image assumes a universal value.

91 · PAUL CEZANNE

Aix-en-Provence, born 1839, died 1906

STILL LIFE

Canvas. Height 18½ in.; width 22 in.

PHILLIPS MEMORIAL GALLERY, WASHINGTON

Claude Monet, the leader of the Impressionists, owned the picture, probably executed between 1895 and 1900. It then passed to the Joseph Stransky collection, New York, before entering the Phillips collection.

A vase covered with straw and some fruit on a table gave a subject matter often repeated by Cézanne in paintings which are quite different from each other, in spite of the fact that they represent the same things. One must emphasize that the subject matter and the vision of the artist are two different things. If the objects represented are alone taken into consideration, we would not find any interest in this picture, which is known as a masterpiece of Cézanne. Until the XIX century the human figure was considered the best subject matter for painting; during the XIX century landscape painting acquired more and more importance. But a still life, in spite of Chardin, never was considered worthy as anything more than to permit a display of ability in the reproduction of nature. A landscape was considered to embody a state of mind; but an apple?

It was indeed Cézanne who impressed a new value on the kind of painting called still life. This was the consequence of that detachment from the subject matter, of that reduction of subject matter to motif, that the Impressionists had initiated. If the subject matter chosen was the most indifferent, casual and common, the problem of style alone became important.

The style was the same as for the Mount Sainte Victoire (No. 90). It lay, that is, in the order of the sensation, in the form of the color masses. But in the landscape the effect was complicated by the distance, the numerous planes, the relation between decoration and construction. On the contrary in our Still Life the problem was very simple: a table, a cloth, some fruit, some pieces of pottery, and a background. Such simplicity was an opportunity and at the same time a difficulty for the creation of a style. The objects were very close to the spectator and could not be oversimplified like a house in a landscape. Style and representation were thus in dangerous contradiction. To overcome this a full artistic realization was necessary, to convince the observer that the product of imagination (style) was as alive as the product of nature (apple).

It is known that Cézanne complained that he could not "realize." His underestimate of his own abilities consisted in the fact that he did not distinguish theoretically between the artistic realization, that is, the expression of his vision and feeling, and the practical realization, that is the illusion of reality.

Cézanne, however, obtained his earliest successes with still life, because with a still life he could give to the public evidence that he was powerful and convincing in both artistic and practical realization. Certainly he did not indulge in an effort to produce the illusion of reality, but the power of his style was such that it suggested even this illusion.

How he did this is clear. The contrasts of tones allow each object represented to impose itself on the imagination of the spectator, with full individuality, in spite of its participation to the ensemble. Furthermore the position of each object in the composition is intended to suggest energy. With a few simple accents Cézanne makes a pear, as it were, try to go off the table, as though living and moving. The directions of the movements are outward, centrifugal. Finally he represented his objects not from a single point of view, but from several, thus giving us a more extended vision of the objects than a man can have in reality. All this reveals an intellectual power of organizing form, which is the basis of the qualities of Cézanne's works of art—that is, their certainty, their Olympian calm, their spontaneity and monumentality.

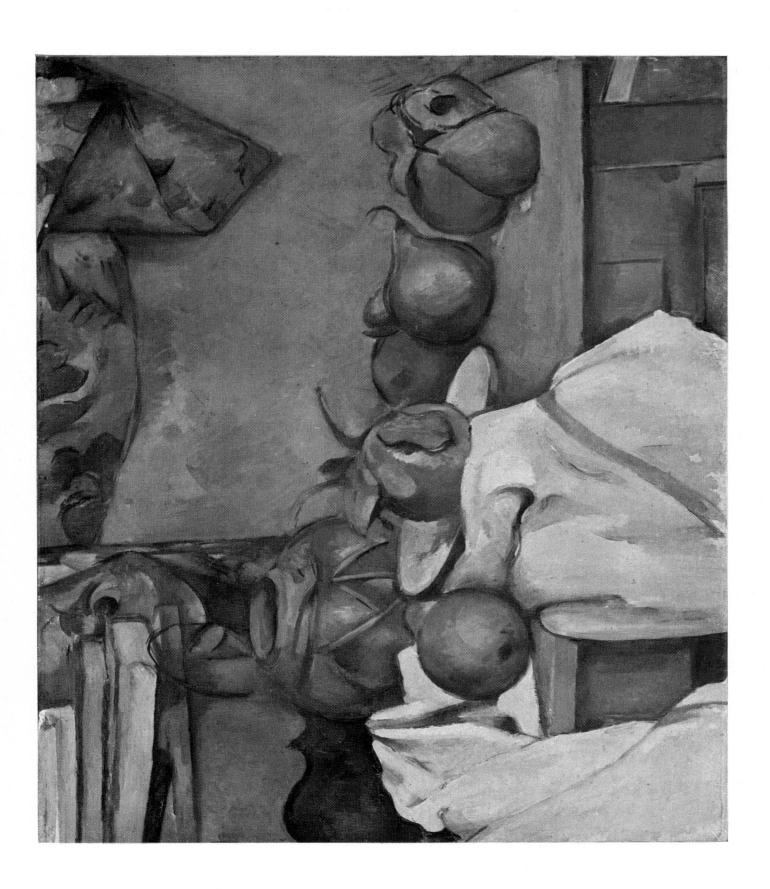

92 · PAUL CÉZANNE

Aix-en-Provence, born 1839, died 1906

LES GRANDES BAIGNEUSES
Canvas. Height 82 in.; width 98 in.

This painting, which came to Philadelphia from the collection of Auguste and Jean Pellerin, Paris, was the mental absorption of Cézanne for seven years, between 1898 and 1905, as tradition tells us. In the ordinary acceptance of the word it was left unfinished. The canvas is uncovered in some places: in the flesh of the bathers, in the clouds, and elsewhere. But no doubt what Cézanne wanted to say was fully and completely realized.

The idea of a composition of bathers appealed to Cézanne for many years, and he repeated it many times in oil and watercolor, sometimes in paintings of large size like the one at the Barnes Foundation, Merion, or the other in the Lecomte collection, Paris. The Great Bathers here illustrated is the largest of all. This has its importance: Cézanne wanted to create a new kind of wall decoration, where the architectural value would be internal, not external, to the painting. The amplitude of the surface thus contributed to the realization of the architectural ideal.

The motif is clear: the main group of the bathers has a horizontal direction, which is underlined by the foreground, the river and the shore behind it. From this horizontal base some lines of trees rise and converge, to form a pyramid. Two bathers in particular and the poses of the others accompany the direction of the trees. Thus all the images concur in forming the geometrical shape of a pyramid.

Cézanne did not want to inscribe his composition in a pyramid, he wanted to form his ideal pyramid with his images. Thus he created it through color zones instead of through lines. The ground, the bathers and the trees all become an ideal pyramid; they are all in brown-orange. The complementary blues, near or far, suggest the atmosphere in which the motif is immersed; they transform the ideal shape into a pictorial ensemble where surface and depth are interwoven.

A detail well reveals Cézanne's aim. The face of the bather second from the left is abridged: her face would have interrupted the back of another bather in the second plane, to paint it in its full proportions would have been a mistake. Cézanne effectively abolished the face, he did not finish the image, but he completed the composition; he did not represent all the elements of nature, but he perfected his work of art. This is the freedom of his imagination.

He painted this great composition in the last years of his life, when he combined, towards a superior synthesis, all the experiences of his creativity; the romantic magic realism of his early period, the sensibility to light and colors of his impressionistic years, the intellectual organization which gave a structural order to his color masses and transformed painting into an ideal architecture. All these experiences were present to the mind of Cézanne when he painted the Great Bathers. His aim was to paint an ideal architecture, but he could not renounce his lively sensibility to colors and tones, nor the romantic mood of the early days. Hence a unity of form and color, an anxious participation in the life of the images, a romantic pathos. Hence that special greatness which art acquires beyond the material size of the canvas, that sacred monumentality which depends on form instead of on subject matter. The work is a painting, but in looking at it one recalls the whole façade of a cathedral.

93 · GEORGES SEURAT

Paris, born 1859, died 1891

SUNDAY AFTERNOON ON THE ISLAND OF LA GRANDE JATTE

Canvas. Height 81 in.; width 120⅜ in.

HELEN BIRCH BARTLETT MEMORIAL. ART INSTITUTE OF CHICAGO, CHICAGO

In 1884, when he was twenty-five years old, Seurat had just finished The Bathers (National Gallery, London). He then conceived a representation of life on Sunday at La Grande Jatte, an island in the Seine near Neuilly which was a popular gathering place on holidays. The same year he exhibited some sketches for it. Working with great care, he exhibited the finished painting in 1886. Daniel Catton Rich, who has studied the development of this painting from the early sketches to the finished work, has listed some fifty sketches and drawings made by Seurat for it. The most important of these is the study in the Lewisohn collection, New York. The painting itself was never sold by Seurat. It remained in the possession of Lucie Cousturier, herself a painter as well as a disciple, promoter of Seurat's fame. Frederic Clay Bartlett bought it from her and gave it to the Art Institute of Chicago.

When the painting was exhibited at the sixth and last exhibition of the Impressionists in 1886, and later at the Society of Independent Artists, it caused a scandal. Nevertheless, many became aware that something new had appeared in the history of taste. Seurat immediately achieved great renown, and a strong influence on the young painters. "Pointillism" and symbolic form found their origin in this painting, which can be considered a turning point of modern art.

From the Impressionists Seurat had learned indifference to the representation of a subject, as well as the love of landscape, and the choice of light as the leading factor of vision. But he reacted against Impressionism in that he wanted to follow not natural sensation but mathematical, scientific reason. He said: "Certain critics see some poetry in my work, I paint according to my method, with no other consideration." We are fortunate that Seurat was a greater artist than theorist. Although he rigorously applied his method, his imagination soared in spite of himself, revealing an ecstatic vision of the world, like that of a child, and ignoring the theories which the method of Seurat sought to exemplify on his canvas.

The general composition of Sunday Afternoon on the Island of La Grande Jatte is a superposition of color zones, where figures are scattered following perspective lines, but with arbitrary proportions which suggest unreality. The dry profiles of the figures accentuate their immobility. The dresses are faithful to the fashion of the time, but by a certain exaggeration and by the addition of umbrellas, dogs, and a monkey, a touch of humor is introduced. The result is a mixture of illusionary appearance and geometric abstractions, of realization and ideology—contrasts which are appeased by the contemplation of an unreal, fantastic world.

The theory of Seurat consists of two parts. The first one concerns the division of tones, previously known by the Impressionists as an experience of the senses, and now systematized by Seurat following the scientific researches of Chevreul, Rood and Sutter. Such systematic use of divided tones was pointillism, that is, a series of small brush strokes giving the illusion of light. The second part of the theory considers the relation between states of mind and dominant tones or directions of lines. For example, sadness is expressed by cold tones and descending lines. All this has no importance in aesthetics; it is not a system of ideas. Its importance lies in the fact that Seurat, who was a very timid man, found in what he considered a system of ideas, the necessary support; the illusion of an indisputable certainty, and was thus able to let his imagination transcend it.

Seurat's imagination, however, was of a new kind, dependent on the need for a theory, on the pretense of refraining from sensibility, on a new adoration for abstract intellectualism. In this sense his theory as well as his painting are the forerunners of abstract art.

94 · PAUL GAUGUIN

Paris, born 1848, died 1903

THE SPIRIT OF THE DEAD WATCHING

Canvas. Height 28¾ in.; width 36¼ in.

A. CONGER GOODYEAR, NEW YORK

This painting, signed and dated 1892, was first commented on by Gauguin himself. He was then living in a hut at Tahiti, in a wholly savage country. One day he had to go to the town of Papeete and returned to his hut in the middle of night. He saw Tehura "immobile, naked, lying on her belly on the bed, with eyes enormously opened by fear. She looked at me and seemed not to recognize me. A contagious influence spread from her fears, it seemed to me that a phosphorescent light came out of her fixed eyes. Never had I seen her so beautiful and so moving." This strong impression is the origin of the painting and explains its vividness as well as its rank among his masterpieces. As for the ideas he followed, he wrote: "The musical part: undulating horizontal lines, harmonies of orange and blue woven together by yellows and violets, their complementary colors, and lightened by greenish sparkles. The literary part: the Spirit of a Living Girl united with the Spirit of the Dead—Night and Day. This explanation of the genesis of my picture is written for the benefit of those who always insist on knowing the why and wherefore of everything. Otherwise it is simply no more than a study of the nude in Oceania."

What Gauguin embodied in his painting but not in his thought, was that his study of a nude was born of the extraordinary impression he described, of his love for savage life, his distrust of civilized life, and his participation in the superstitions of the savages. Neither his colors nor his forms, his composition nor his motif could be explained by the civilization he had left behind in Paris. He had sacrificed his well-being and that of his family, and was even slowly destroying his very life, in order to live in that atmosphere of dreams and fears, at that door opened on the unknown, which was then a wood at Tahiti.

His main desire was to find a type of painting which could satisfy him. He had been a follower of Pissarro, at the moment of the crisis of Impressionism, and realized that something new was necessary. For a while he profited from the constructive trend of Cézanne, but the painting of Cézanne was too complex and required a mind too intellectual ultimately to attract Gauguin.

Ganguin began to simplify his tones in order to use more intense colors, to simplify the planes in order to emphasize the values of the surface, to renounce direct study from nature in order to create decorative compositions. Furthermore, around 1890, he became a friend of the Symbolist poets and, being highly praised by them, he aspired to be a Symbolist painter.

What Gauguin gave as a gift to the tradition of art, however, was an enormous expansion of the concept of art, which he liberated from too many ties with the conventions of Parisian society. Of course Cézanne had also done this; but, by putting the accent on the savage and by carrying the effort to its extreme consequences, Gauguin opened the way to the understanding of less civilized arts, which are now commonly accepted. Moreover, by stressing the importance of decoration, of the surface in painting, of pure and intense colors and their harmonies outside chiaroscuro, he contributed to the trend toward abstract art. Finally, he found in simplification of forms a way for that intense expression which was later called expressionism.

Aside from his merits as a prophet in taste, Gauguin achieved a few, though not very many, great works of art. These appeared when he participated in his motifs with all his senses and with a concentrated imagination. The Spirit of the Dead Watching is beyond any doubt one of the finest of his creations.

95 · VINCENT VAN GOGH

Groot-Zundert in Brabant, born 1853, died 1891

L'ARLÉSIENNE (MADAME GINOUX)

Canvas. Height 36 in.; width 29 in.

SAM. A. LEWISOHN, NEW YORK

In November, 1888, Van Gogh painted this portrait of the wife of M. Ginoux, the proprietor of a coffee house near the railroad station at Arles, where the painter used to pass his hours of leisure. He was attracted both by the exotic appearance of the woman and by her costume — and he was satisfied with his work. He wrote to his brother: "Then I have an Arlésienne at last, a figure slashed on in an hour, background pale lemon, the face grey, the clothes black, black, black, with perfectly raw Prussian blue. She is leaning on a green table and seated in an armchair of orange wood." Later he wrote: "I am pleased too to hear that someone else has turned up who actually saw something in the woman's figure, in black and yellow. That does not surprise me, though I think that the merit is in the model and not in my painting." These letters tell us a great deal about Van Gogh's conception of coloring, and his modesty.

Since the XV century, no painter had so thoroughly excluded chiaroscuro, or the effect of light and shade, as did Van Gogh. He wrote that he wanted to insist on pure colors, abstracted from reality, in order to express himself more freely. The blues of the dress and the hair oppose themselves to the yellow of the background like shade against light, but in a purely symbolic way. A symbol in art being a generalization, the contrast of Van Gogh's colors does not create an effect of light. But the image assumes an energy which forcibly strikes the observer.

Colors without an effect of light cannot build up a volume, but offer a succession of flat zones and call for a shape rather than a form. Under the inspiration of Japanese prints, and aided by the unusual costume of the women of Arles, Van Gogh achieved a shape which is somewhat whimsical and fantastic yet attractive and felicitous.

His abstract vision of color zones thoroughly realizes a natural image and convinces us that both natural image and artistic vision were born together. The artist has created a new vision of reality, different from what we see, but as convincing as visual reality itself, and coinciding with it in the infinite. This is the physical beauty of the image, and its value as pure art.

Van Gogh was the son of a Protestant minister from whom he inherited his great desire to preach in everything he attempted—in business, in religion, in social reform, in his private life, as well as in his art. This zeal for reforming corresponds to an excess of emotion. As long as he remained within the limits of his Dutch training in painting, which was traditional and academic, his emotions were too strong to be realized in the forms he had learned. But after settling in Paris in 1886, and becoming acquainted with Impressionism, above all with the Symbolism of Gauguin at its dawn, Van Gogh was able to free himself from what he had learned and create a form of his own. It was indeed his simplification of form and color, his renunciation of relief and of light and shade, which allowed him to concentrate his emotions in form and color. His emotionality, his spirit of self-sacrifice and adoration—an adoration for everything he loved—peasants and trees, as well as his masters—enabled him to vitalize color zones which otherwise would have been merely decorative. He believed that the beauty of the Arlésienne was due to the model. Because of this modesty, because of his faith in the object, he was able to offer modern and contemporary taste not only new decorative motifs but also the expression of a profound life, which constitutes the greatness of his art.

96 · VINCENT VAN GOGH

Groot-Zundert in Brabant, born 1853, died 1891

THE STARRY NIGHT

Canvas. Height 29 in.; width 36¼ in.

MUSEUM OF MODERN ART, NEW YORK

One month after his arrival at Saint-Rémy, where he had retired in order to cure his sporadic mental disorders, Van Gogh wrote to his brother, in June, 1889: "Finally I painted a landscape with olive trees and also a new study of a starry sky." The latter is The Starry Night, which came to the Museum of Modern Art from the collection of Miss G. P. van Stolk, Rotterdam. The letter continues: "It is not a return to romanticism or to religious ideas. However, through a greater experience of Delacroix than it would appear, through more subjective colors and forms than the imitation of nature allows, one could express the nature of a country more purified than that of the suburbs of Paris. One could also paint human beings more serene and pure than those Daumier had before his eyes, without renouncing his kind of drawing . . . perhaps when we read Zola we are moved by the music of a purer French style, like for example that of Renan."

This is the program not of a mad man but of a seer, and it reveals the intimate source of the creation of The Starry Night. Van Gogh had burnt out his own life in order to reach an artistic reality linked with his every day life of misery and sorrow. From an asylum, when everything seemed lost to him, he aspired to a purer world than the one he knew, a world morally sound and artistically serene. The contemplation of a starry night, nothing better, to evoke a pure ecstasy.

At Saint-Rémy Van Gogh was well pleased; he looked at the landscape and found enjoyment. He had emerged from his previous struggles and disorders, and poetry came naturally with his colors. "Cypresses interest me continuously, I should like to paint them like my sunflowers. I am indeed surprised that nobody has seen them as I do. Their lines and proportions are beautiful as an Egyptian obelisk . . . One must see them against the blue, or, better, immersed in the blue." When Van Gogh painted cypresses he could not represent their geometric shape, their obelisk form, he saw them as flames aspiring to the heavens. In The Starry Night flames are in the foreground, they represent a cypress. The sky, too, is burning; rivers of fire travel over it along curved lines and large or small explosions stand for the stars. Below is the dark blue landscape. It is a vision of a cosmic fire, which reveals the fire of Van Gogh's soul.

It is a fantastic vision, but it is far from pure fancy. In his vision Van Gogh concentrates not only his exceptional power as a colorist, but also his emotionality, his adoration for what he sees, his sense of mystery, his longing for the unknown.

Van Gogh's magic is the result of pure colors, because he impresses each of his colors with his burning love. His form, likewise, is perfectly appropriate to his colors, that is, it is a shape of elements, always in movement, with contours sometimes interrupted, sometimes continuous, always vibrating and full of life. Perhaps he could not achieve what we consider serenity, but we must realize that there exists a serenity which is a balance between effort and sorrow—it is the escape from misery, the daring journey towards the unknown, the realization of a cosmic tragedy.

97 · HENRI DE TOULOUSE-LAUTREC

Albi, born 1864, died 1901

AT THE MOULIN ROUGE: THE DANCE

Canvas. Height 45¼ in.; width 59 in.

HENRY P. MCILHENNY, PHILADELPHIA

For some years this picture, signed and dated 1890, hung above the bar at the entrance to the dance-hall of the Moulin Rouge. Later, it came into the possession of Mr. McIlhenny from the Sévadjian collection, Paris.

This is the earliest of the paintings illustrating the Moulin Rouge, the night-club which was the preferred place of observation and inspiration for Toulouse-Lautrec between 1890 and 1896. It represents Valentin le Désossé dancing the quadrille with his partner in the presence of the customary clients. Among them are portrayed, in the background at the right of Valentin, Jane Avril, Maurice Guibert, the photographer Paul Sescau and the painter François Gauzi.

Youngest among the great masters of the XIX century, Lautrec represented in a striking way that sad "gaiety" which was typical of the *fin de siècle*. He resumed and made fashionable the tradition of illustration, which had been ignored by the Impressionists, and worked out a unity of illustration and decoration in his posters, which are perhaps the most artistic posters ever done. He simplified his form, renouncing plasticity, accentuating contours, and expanding colors in flat zones, in order to emphasize the meaning of the scene and to arrange for a decorative effect.

Both his grotesque interpretation of human forms and his decorative fancy took Lautrec beyond any realism, towards a form appropriate for an unsound and artificial world. In contrast with the love for the open country displayed by the Impressionists and Cézanne, and the longing of Gauguin for barbarous, virgin land, Lautrec preferred the vitiated atmosphere of the night-clubs, the "cafés-concerts" and the "maisons closes." He knew perfectly that vice is mournful, and he did not conceal this; on the contrary, he exhibited it as it was, with a touch of viciousness even in the ornaments of a hat or a wall.

He drew the portrait of the Parisian *demi-monde* of his time, and did even more: he gave a style to the life of this circle. His sympathy for that life depended on his imaginative pleasure. He was neither a moralist, nor did he profit by vice—he looked at it and enjoyed playing with it in order to create a new style. Even the perfect form of vice can be art, if it is disinterested.

Lautrec belonged to one of the greatest noble families of France and was destined for a leisurely and whimsical life, when his legs, broken as a child, transformed him into a kind of monster. He could not remain in his own milieu. He acquiesced in being cast out, and found himself at home among other outcasts. This is the reason why he represented the *demi-monde* without irony and without disguise, with a full participation in its life.

He was trained in academic drawing, but he felt how false was its ideal. Hence he directed himself towards the opposite, the deformed and the comic. A great tradition, that of Goya and Daumier, helped him. He became a forerunner of expressionism.

In the gay life of the 'nineties we see only mourning, and in the drawing, or coloring, or composition of Lautrec's paintings we find but a limited interest. But his state of mind, his desperate adhesion to the life of the outcast, his ability to give a style to it, create something heroic which is still alive, and is a unique sort of poetry.

98 · PABLO PICASSO

Malaga, born 1881

BOY LEADING A HORSE

Canvas. Height 86½ in.; width 51¼ in.

WILLIAM S. PALEY, NEW YORK

The year 1905, when Picasso painted this picture, is one of the happiest for his art, and this picture is one of the masterpieces of that year. Today we are accustomed to associate the name of Picasso with the terrific experiences of the last decades in the field of art: cubism, surrealism, expressionism, and so on. In 1905 Picasso was doing a very wise kind of painting of which everyone recognizes the results as works of art, even judging by traditional ideas. Of course this is not an academic painting, but it can be justified by academic standards, as can, for example, the works of Puvis de Chavannes.

Picasso made many efforts before bringing to conclusion the Boy Leading a Horse. One can see his drawings and sketches with the same motif in plates 118, 119 and 120 of Zervos' "Pablo Picasso" (vol. I). The form and the attitude of the horse were reached at once. But the boy was studied at half and entire figure, dressed and naked, leaning on a parapet or walking. The artist also, under the influence of Degas, imagined a composition with various horses and boys. The final picture, however, has no longer any relation either to Degas or to Puvis de Chavannes; it shows the personality of Picasso exclusively. In the sketches one can see the nervous and interrupted drawing which includes an effect of light and shade and recalls Picasso's previous experience of the art of Toulouse-Lautrec and of Symbolism generally. But in the final picture, of all these tentatives, there remains only a vibrating sensibility underneath a classic form. The fact that the gesture of the boy is justified by his appearing to hold the bridle of the horse, but that the bridle is not represented, is a detail which demonstrates clearly how Picasso ignores representation in order to emphasize the presentation of images.

The ideal of the painter is to realize a formal beauty in physical bodies, and the value of the mind is limited to the vividness and the distinction of that formality. If we now recall the whole trend of painting in modern times, from Delacroix through Daumier and Cézanne, to Gauguin and Van Gogh, we become aware that the ideal of Picasso is very different from that of all of them, and closer to the academic tradition.

When this statement is made, one usually hears an expression of surprise, in view of the changing ideals of Picasso, who one year after the Boy Leading a Horse began *Les Demoiselles d'Avignon*, starting his adventure through Negro sculpture towards Cubism. However when we understand the intimate coherence of Picasso's art, we are aware that the many changes, which are numerous indeed, obey the necessity felt by the artist of attaining formal abstraction.

Picasso approached abstraction from many directions, but one thing remained constant: his generalized content, his vague understanding of the life of feeling, and his sure and overpowering preoccupation with physical bodies. His paintings, both representative and non-representative, objective and non-objective, belong in a rarefied atmosphere, in the physical as well as in the moral sense of the word. Fanciful images appear without any other reason but their very appearance. Thus the Boy Leading a Horse is the announcement of the Picasso to come.

99 · HENRI MATISSE

Le Cateau near St. Quentin, born 1869

THE BLUE WINDOW

Canvas. Height 51½ in.; width 35⅝ in.

MUSEUM OF MODERN ART, NEW YORK

If the Boy Leading a Horse by Picasso (no. 98) can be considered an early manifestation of the modern trend towards an abstract form, The Blue Window by Matisse, painted around 1912, is a perfect early example of the ideal of pure color to which plastic form is subordinated.

Nothing can better help us to understand the creative process of Matisse than to quote his own words: "Suppose I set out to paint an interior: I have before me a cupboard; it gives me a sensation of bright red and I put down a red which satisfies me; immediately a relation is established between this red and the white of the canvas. If I put a green near the red, if I paint a yellow floor, there must still be between this green this yellow and the white of the canvas a relation that will be satisfactory to me. But these several tones mutually weaken one another. It is necessary, therefore, that the various elements that I use be so balanced that they do not destroy one another ... A new combination of colors will supersede the first one and will give my interpretation more completely. I am forced to transpose until finally my picture may seem completely changed when, after successive modifications, the red has succeeded the green as the dominant color." This is a perfect description of the process which transforms a physical sensation into an imaginative painting, that is, into an original creation of Matisse's own form of colors.

Some consequences of such a creative process are clear in The Blue Window. Above all, the objects are represented by patterns, not by plastic forms; at most a reflection of light in the glass vase of flowers suggest its depth. In other words, the representation of things is purely symbolic, transforming them into their phantasms.

Furthermore, the whole composition emphasizes the surface at the expense of the third dimension. There is a hint of space behind the objects, but it is a composition of space which is purely symbolic, an indication, not a representation. Finally, no movement is suggested in the various patterns. Because movement is always merely suggestive of actual life, the static appearances of The Blue Window remain a presentation and not a representation.

The artistic life of the painting is thus abstract from reality, it begins beyond reality. The elements of reality, the vase of flowers, a tree in a garden, a cloud in the sky, do not exist for the work of art. What exists is a composition of colors and patterns, fabulous colors which are a creation of the mind and do not exist in reality, and fantastic patterns which are justified only by their colors and by their position on the surface. And what of the content? It is a dream of an unknown world, a fairy-tale about unseen phantasms. This is the contribution given to the harmony of colors and patterns by the humanity of Matisse.

Matisse has a highly intellectual mind. As a critic he controls his own work, but he knows that control must begin only after creation. This deliberate detachment of his intellect from his artistic creation is the reason for the purity of his art, for its coherence, its primitivism and its spontaneity, but also for the thinness of its human interest. No religious, no social, no dramatic feeling can be discovered in his work. But he makes up for this narrowness by his purity. Within his own world, made of enchanting colors and patterns, his fancy has no limits. Everywhere his fancy reaches, there is creation.

It has often been said that Matisse's art is decorative rather than expressive. To say this is false aesthetics. Matisse's paintings have a content very different from that of other painters, a narrow one, but it exists. Otherwise he would not express anything. On the contrary, the perfect choice of his motifs, adapted to his form and hence revealed by his form, is one of the glories of Matisse.

100 · GEORGES ROUAULT

Paris, born 1871

THE OLD KING

Canvas. Height 30¼ in.; width 21¼ in.

To understand Picasso the guiding element is abstract form, to understand Matisse, it is abstract color. To understand Rouault the present religious trends and social reactions in France are as important as his colors and forms. After having become a master of academic painting, in 1903 he rebelled against the academic tradition as well as against the evils of Parisian life. Leon Bloy, a religious reformer, who preferred Christian barbarity to Christian civilization, influenced Rouault, who created in painting some "monsters" in order to strike against the evils of civilization. For some ten years he continued to fight with his brushes, inducing scandal after scandal, and achieving a style of caricature where the comic and the sublime were woven together. His religious mood imprinted on his caricatures an unexpected grandeur and energy, and he became the greatest polemic in painting of his time.

Then came the first world war and a period in which Rouault dedicated himself almost exclusively to the illustration of books. Only about 1929 did he resume his painting. Often he reworked his old sketches, making painting upon painting, in order to deepen their pictorial quality. There is no doubt that this falling back on his own creations, often after a lapse of many years, served to intensify the life of his canvases. The thickness of his impasto has no other origin than this. Rouault does not obtain the vitality of his pictures by his renewed vision of nature but by a superposition of tones each more elaborate than the other. At the basis of the sketch there is a natural motive; in the finished work his relation to nature is three or four degrees further removed. The more remote its affinity to nature becomes, the greater the proximity to imagination.

The Old King was begun in 1916 and completed in 1936. It summarizes the quality of Rouault's paintings. His coloring is unique, not only very intense, but also in a way phosphorescent. It seems, indeed, not to receive light from outside, but to spread a kind of fanciful light by itself. His form is based on the juxtaposition of zones of color outlined by large touches of black. This has suggested a comparison with medieval stained glass, but the blacks of Rouault have a pictorial value unknown to the Middle Ages. Moreover, his form is not flat, but because of the underlying drawing suggests strong volumes. Finally, his expression is of an exceptional strength, with a severity, a determination, a fabulous dignity. It is as though the whole sorrow of mankind were concentrated in The Old King.

In this picture polemics have disappeared. Rouault has not renounced any of his convictions, but through the years he has detached himself not only from reality, but also from the moral evils he hates. Of his old caricatures he has retained only the form, which the caricatures suggested to him, but which is now independent. Thus after 1930 he found his own style, one of an incredible richness and coherence. Hence his masterpieces, among which The Old King is commanding.

101 · JOHN MARIN
Rutherford, New Jersey, born 1870

LOWER MANHATTAN
Watercolor on paper. Height 21⅞ in.; width 26⅞ in.

There is a statement written by Marin in 1913 for an exhibition at Alfred Stieglitz' place called "291" which sets forth the mood that likewise inspired Lower Manhattan, a painting of 1920.

"The later pictures of New York shown in this exhibition may need the help of an explanation," it reads. "These few words are written to quicken your response to my point of view.

"Shall we consider the life of a great city as confined simply to the people and animals on its streets and in its buildings? Are the buildings themselves dead? We have been told somewhere that a work of art is a thing alive. You cannot create a work of art unless the things you behold respond to something within you. Therefore if these buildings move me they too must have life. Thus the whole city is alive; buildings, people, all are alive; and the more they move me the more I feel them to be alive.

"It is this 'moving of me' that I try to express, so that I may recall the spell I have been under and behold the expression of the different emotions that have been called into being. How am I to express what I feel so that its expression will bring me back under the spell? Shall I copy facts photographically?

"I see great forces at work; great movements; the large buildings and the small buildings; the warring of the great and the small; influences of one mass on another greater or smaller mass. Feelings are aroused which give me the desire to express the reaction of these 'pull forces,' those influences which play with one another; great masses pulling smaller masses, each subject in some degree to the other's power.

"In life all things come under the magnetic influence of other things: the bigger assert themselves strongly, the smaller not so much, but still they assert themselves, and though hidden they strive to be seen and in so doing change their bent and direction.

"While these powers are at work pushing, pulling, sideways, downwards, upwards, I can hear the sound of their strife and there is great music being played.

"And so I try to express graphically what a great city is doing. Within the frames there must be a balance, a controlling of these warring, pushing, pulling forces. This is what I am trying to realize. But we are all human."

Marin loves the sea, the mountains and sailboats, whatever is in the open air, whatever is simple, natural, without sophistication. If he is attracted also by skyscrapers and elevated railways, it is by their daring, by their dynamics, by some sort of diabolic power which is in them. This adhesion to the motif is so close that we see his reality quite clearly and almost forget that his form is abstract.

When Marin went to Paris in 1905 he etched under the influence of Whistler and painted under that of Monet. But after 1908 he felt the spell of the new visualization in painting, due to the Fauves and the Cubists. He profited by the lesson, freeing his watercolors from any interference of objective nature. Thus, for example, he understood that a building in painting must sacrifice even its stability to show its expressive power.

There is nothing arbitrary in his painting; he is absorbed in his vision with such intensity that every touch of his is in the right place, where it is necessary and significant. His reality is that of a vision, even, if you like, that of a fantastic vision. But its coherence being absolute, the whole acquires a unity, which is life, parallel to nature, and natural as nature itself.

Marin's ideal is one of coordination, of balance, and of structure. The lively intensity of his painting reflects his own intensity of feeling; hence the sense of reality he gives. He mocks the painters who say they represent their inner vision instead of the things seen: "If you have an intense love and feeling towards these things, you'll try your dam'dest to put on paper or canvas that thing; you can transpose, you can play with and on your material, but when you are finished, that's got to have the roots of that thing in it and no other thing." It is his devotion to nature, his modesty before nature, which give Marin power for his kind of realization. For this American painter it is a paradoxical privilege, but a great privilege, that he paints abstraction and represents reality.

216